THE BUSINESS OF CREATIVITY

PUBLISHED BY PRINCETON ARCHITECTURAL PRESS
A McEVOY GROUP COMPANY
37 EAST 7TH STREET, NEW YORK, NEW YORK 10003
WWW.PAPRESS.COM

ISBN: 978-1-61689-394-1

EDITOR: SARA STEMEN   DESIGNER: BENJAMIN ENGLISH

SPECIAL THANKS TO: JANET BEHNING, NICOLA BROWER,
ABBY BUSSEL, ERIN CAIN, TOM CHO, BARBARA DARKO,
JENNY FLORENCE, JAN CIGLIANO HARTMAN, LIA HUNT,
MIA JOHNSON, VALERIE KAMEN, SIMONE KAPLAN-SENCHAK,
STEPHANIE LEKE, DIANE LEVINSON, JENNIFER LIPPERT,
KRISTY MAIER, SARA McKAY, JAIME NELSON NOVEN,
ROB SHAEFFER, PAUL WAGNER, JOSEPH WESTON, AND
JANET WONG OF PRINCETON ARCHITECTURAL PRESS
— KEVIN C. LIPPERT, PUBLISHER

IMAGE CREDITS: 8, PHOTOGRAPH BY KEITH GRANET. 99, 100,
COURTESY OF DESIGNERSAXIS SOCIAL MEDIA. 105, COURTESY
OF SUZANNE KASLER. 106, COURTESY OF GP SCHAFER ARCHI-
TECT. 107, COURTESY OF TOM STRINGER DESIGN PARTNERS.
108, COURTESY OF STUDIO WILLIAM HEFNER. 109, COURTESY
OF McALPINE. 161, PHOTOGRAPH BY JOSH GRANET

LIBRARY OF CONGRESS CATALOGING-IN-PUBLICATION DATA
IS AVAILABLE ON REQUEST FROM THE PUBLISHER.

THE
Business
OF
Creativity

HOW TO
BUILD THE RIGHT TEAM
FOR SUCCESS

Keith Granet

PRINCETON ARCHITECTURAL PRESS, NEW YORK

To my clients.

You gave me your sandboxes to explore and your firms to grow.

We experimented, we learned, and together we succeeded.

I am blessed to have you in my life.

CONTENTS

Introduction

THE BOOK YOU ARE HOLDING was inspired by my desire to build on my first book, *The Business of Design*, and to help creative people understand that they are not in this world alone—that design, all design, is a collaborative effort. While one creative individual might germinate a design, the success of its execution comes from finding the right support.

During the writing of this book, I had the opportunity while on a business trip to stop for a few days in Santorini, Greece. My hope was that by escaping the day-to-day activities of my job, I would be able to really think about the message I want to send to my readers. Santorini's white buildings with blue accents appear to meet the earth with the symmetry of a well-choreographed dance or to follow the rhythm of a poem that captures your soul. The simplicity of the designs and the imperfections of the architecture, combined with the astonishing blue of the Aegean Sea, are inspiring, especially for anyone involved in the creative process. This timeless place would not exist if its founders' original vision had not been supported by a group of individuals working together who believed this place could and should exist.

In your own practice, developing your ideas, finding the resources to bring them to life, and marketing your designs all depend on the team you build. The details of running your business are often background noise that can keep you up at night worrying. Your goal in the design of your firm is to surround yourself with people who can lower that background noise to give you room for greater creativity. As a creative person, you should understand your business and even be adept at your business. But it is crucial to know what you do best and to stay focused on that. You must understand your own strengths and weaknesses, and you must also understand what you do and don't know.

As the president of Granet & Associates, the firm I started twenty-five years ago to bring good business practices to the design community, I have always said that I am the idea guy and that without my team none of those ideas would see the light of day. When I get wrapped up in the big idea, things still happen because I surround myself with those who truly know how to execute an idea.

Each chapter in this book describes a skill set you will need to maximize your own creativity. You may not need a separate person with each of these skills, but you will need to ensure that each is covered in your organization, whether you are a sole proprietor or you have hundreds of employees or anything in between.

Chapter One is about the financier: the person who understands and manages all your financial resources. Your financier must be worthy of the highest level of trust; too many creative people have lost their way due to finance troubles.

Chapter Two introduces the need for a great negotiator. Many talented people struggle in this area; they love their craft so much that ensuring that their fees match their value is less important. Therefore, if you are not good at negotiation, find someone who can do this for you and who will do it with your voice in mind. This is central to how you communicate the value of your talent.

Chapter Three describes in depth the marketer. In today's world, marketing and public relations are not as simple as aligning yourself with a magazine. All kinds of social media channels and other methods have joined traditional print media outlets as means of bringing exposure to your work. This chapter introduces you to the people who can help promote your work and also will assist you in determining which types of promotion will require your personal focus.

Chapter Four addresses how to build the team of people who will help to realize your ideas. The idea of a team stretches beyond the four walls of our work environment to include all the external people who are valuable resources. These could include a contractor, a furniture maker, or a patron; each of these people will help you to produce your best work.

Chapter Five is titled "The People You *Don't* Need in Your Life." Too many people tolerate the wrong people in their work—people whose vision is not aligned with their own mission. We have all experienced bad clients and bad employees and bad relationships. The trick to handling these relationships is to recognize when they are not working and to move away from them as quickly as possible. This chapter will help you to identify the wrong people and understand why they need to leave and how to let them go.

Chapter Six articulates the things that you can do to bring your talent to life. All of the other chapters emphasize delegating work to someone else; this chapter points out the tasks and skills that must come only from you. This chapter will help you to evaluate your own skill set and strengths as a way of defining your role and determining which responsibilities belong only to you.

The Business of Creativity is meant to give you the tools to build the best platform for your talents. Whether you are reading this because you want to maximize your talents or you are the person supporting someone with great talent, my hope is that this book will become your guide to achieving something wonderful in your career.

CHAPTER ONE

The Financier: Protecting Your Investment

Why Your Finances Matter

IF THE BRAIN of a design firm is the principal's creative abilities and aesthetic acumen, then strong financial practices and clear accounting procedures are its beating heart and flowing circulatory system. The blood and air are the money that keeps your firm going and growing; when that money isn't moving correctly (or isn't moving at all) because your systems are broken (or, even worse, were never put in place), your firm may manage to survive, but it certainly won't thrive.

This chapter will help you thrive. The following pages are about monetizing your creativity: teaching you how to value yourself, your work, and your firm and how to make sure you get paid for that value. But your firm's finances go well beyond such obviously monetary matters as profit and loss (P&L), how cash moves around, and your bottom line. A company that's functioning well financially will have put in place a suite of systems—and a staff of people—that ensure stability, encourage success, and allow for growth. This certainly includes P&L, but it also encompasses everything from budgeting to business alliances, client contracting to employee benefits, fee structure to insurance coverage.

The firms that meet with the most lasting success are those whose principals really and truly pay attention to their finances—establishing goals and budgets, setting up tracking systems, and reviewing and analyzing financial statements on a regular basis. These firms thrive, even in down markets; they remain nimble, and therefore sustainable, during the most difficult economic times. And they're also the ones that are most able to expand and diversify in good times.

In fact, I've even seen firms with mediocre talent but great business practices meet with tremendous success. I'd be hard-pressed, however, to point to a firm that's truly succeeded when the opposite was true; you may be the world's most talented designer, but without strong financial systems behind you, without strategic planning of your money and operations, you're in for a bumpy, and not particularly lucrative, ride.

The strategies and tactics laid out in this chapter are as vital to your firm as your creativity—at times, they may be even more important.

WHY A STARVING ARTIST HELPS NO ONE

I know what you're thinking. You didn't become a designer because you like finance or business—or even math. You became a designer because you're creative and highly visual; you have great taste and style. You're an artist.

But understanding your finances, establishing a budget, setting up systems to track your business, and hiring the right staff won't sacrifice your creativity or make you any less of an artist. If anything, these practices will give you more time and space in which to be creative, because your firm will be in a stable position and you won't spend nearly as much time worrying about its solvency. With financial security comes creative freedom.

And yet, the romantic myth of the starving artist persists.

In large part, this is because creatives would all too often gladly do what they do for free. It's their passion and their love, and they're so happy to do it, they feel almost as if they don't have to be paid for it. It's as if being creative were at odds with making money.

But it's not—at least it doesn't have to be. And that's a very good thing, because just being happy doesn't pay your rent or keep the lights on—or pay the salaries of your staff, even if you have just one person working with you.

What you do with your creative talent has value, extreme value, for your clients. (Just ask any amateur who's tried to build a house or decorate a home without any help and met with disastrous—and expensive—results.) You need to own that and firmly believe that you have every right to be paid, and paid well.

How often have you seen a starving artist build a practice, let alone oversee a mightily successful one? If you're not charging people, you can't employ people. If you're starving, you can't have a firm that grows. Setting up financial systems and strategies and hiring financial staff are crucial to achieving that growth.

Your Finance Team

I'm not asking you to look after your firm's finances by yourself. Far from it, in fact. Without question, you need to have oversight and ultimate responsibility—because the buck stops with you. But the key thing is for you to have finance people, whether on staff or off, who can look after the day-to-day accounting and then provide you with easy-to-understand information on a regular basis. At first, this will probably be a part-time bookkeeper. As your firm grows, the role will likely expand to a full-time, on-staff bookkeeper, then perhaps a controller and then a CFO or director of finance. When your firm is large enough, you may have a finance staff of several people, with a bookkeeper or assistant handling data entry to support the controller or CFO, as well as someone just overseeing accounts payable, another overseeing accounts receivable, and still another handling payroll.

WHY YOU BUILD A TEAM

You need to hire financial people for the simple reason that you need to take finances off your plate. Many people try to handle their own finances, however. They start their business knowing how to create an invoice and send it off to a client, and they get a computer program like QuickBooks and try to set up their own accounting and financial systems. But very quickly they start to struggle.

Even at that point, designers may resist hiring someone with expertise because doing so seems like an added expense. In the long run, however, it will save you money, both because it will prevent errors and because it will save you the time you would otherwise spend on it. And that allows you to earn money working on actual creative projects, instead of wasting time wrestling with QuickBooks—and worrying. If you're spending ten hours a week doing your finances—and another ten worrying about them—you

> "Work slowly and work with people who share your values, whether they're employees, clients, or colleagues." **MARK FERGUSON**

are squandering time better spent designing for your clients. They pay you for that time, and that means you can well afford the cost of someone to do your books.

You shouldn't be doing your books for the same reason your clients shouldn't hire an accountant to design their homes. Expertise breeds success.

WHO'S ON THE TEAM

The financial people you will hire will change as your firm and its needs grow. Below are the most common positions, starting with those you'll want during the earliest and smallest days of your firm, up through a time when your company is well established and quite large, with significantly more sophisticated needs.

Part-Time Bookkeeper

This is usually the first finance person you'll bring in, ideally contracting with someone who has experience in the design industry and is familiar with how it works. In addition to doing basic data entry to keep your financial records accurate and up-to-date, a part-time bookkeeper can send bills and contracts out in a timely manner, collect owed fees, and help you review your finances every month. Depending on the person's skill set, you could also ask a part-time bookkeeper to handle payroll, manage your accounting programs and updates, establish vendor accounts, and create office and project budgets. You should expect that a part-time bookkeeper will come to your office at minimum once a week, most likely more frequently during your billing cycle. A firm can generally manage with a part-time bookkeeper until the head count goes over five.

Full-Time Bookkeeper

As your firm grows and becomes more complex, you will need to hire a bookkeeper as part of your in-house team. This person will fulfill the same functions as the part-time independent contractor but will work exclusively for you and therefore will have greater involvement in day-to-day activities, working with your designers on

Job Title: Controller

Reports to: Partners

GENERAL DESCRIPTION

The controller is accountable for overseeing the overall accounting operations of the firm. This hands-on employee manages and administers financial and accounting functions, including management reporting; preparing financial statements, including general ledger reconciliation; project and cost accounting, including budgeting and planning; invoicing; cash management; banking; and managing computer accounting systems. The controller must be skilled in budgeting, forecasting, and analysis in order to assist the partners proactively in assessing the overall financial and administrative health of the company and bringing efficiency to all systems. This employee is responsible for looking at new and more efficient ways of managing the office and making recommendations for change.

SPECIFIC RESPONSIBILITIES

Bookkeeping

Manage accounts payable and receivable, data input, payroll, cash flow, and job costing.

Invoicing & Accounts Receivable

Ensure that all hours and expenses for each project are captured on invoices every month. Create draft fees and expense invoices for partners and project managers to review. Finalize, post, and mail all invoices by the tenth of each month. Make collections calls as per the office collections policy. Print accounts receivable reports for the partners monthly and as needed. Discuss with partners the status of long-outstanding invoices and decide action as per the office collections policy.

Accounts Payable

Manage the consultant and trade payable invoices. Request approvals for vendor and consultant invoices from partners. Process checks.

Payroll

Process payroll and record payroll in accounting system. Provide quarterly and year-end payroll reports to CPA for tax purposes.

Banking

Deposit all cash receipts as they are received. Monitor current cash accounts and ensure that all disbursements are funded. Perform bank reconciliations for all accounts. Transfer funds, with partner authorization.

Human Resources

Give employment and payroll forms to new employees. Administer all employee benefits, including 401(k) accounts, health benefits, insurance policies, and vacation/sick accruals. Liaise with partners regarding benefit costs.

Reporting

Print and analyze month-end financial reports. Print project cost reports for project managers and partners as needed.

General

Ensure the integrity and confidentiality of the accounting office. Implement new upgrades and modules for accounting system as needed.

1.1   Sample job description for a controller

project and office budgets. By being more involved, the full-time bookkeeper will minimize the work that you pay your accountant to do at year's end to prepare your tax returns.

Controller

Once your firm has between twenty and thirty people, it's time to either replace or augment your bookkeeper with someone who has more experience and expertise. A controller is usually a certified public accountant (CPA) with a deep understanding of financial reporting and tax planning. Controllers are more heavily involved in the overall financial management of the firm. They often negotiate vendor and client contracts and become involved in some human resource areas, including employee benefits such as profit sharing, bonus programs, and other perks. **FIG 1.1**

Chief Financial Officer (CFO) or Director of Finance

Your firm may ultimately hire someone who has a forward-looking, business-planning mind-set and broader expertise to build on the planning and accounting activities of your controller. It's usually when a firm has more than thirty employees that this level of senior financial person becomes necessary—and affordable. A CFO, like a controller, will look at every dollar spent and every dollar billed on a monthly basis, but he or she will also think strategically, consulting with you about ways to expand and further monetize the business. This person will usually manage some aspects of human resources, such as payroll and benefits, and will work with the creative principal or principals to create financial goals and budgets. He or she will also help your entire team understand the firm's finances, including each staff member's role in contributing to the bottom line, be it by managing costs or just running projects more efficiently. You can expect this person to be significantly involved in negotiating contracts with clients.

Note that, generally speaking, each of the positions described above is replaced by the one that comes after it, though the more senior employees (controller and

	Chief Financial Officer	Controller	Full-Time Bookkeepr	Part-Time Bookkeeper
Northeast	$ 150,000	100,000	85,000	50/hr.
Southeast	$ 110,000	85,000	75,000	35/hr.
South	$ 115,000	90,000	80,000	40/hr.
Midwest	$ 110,000	85,000	75,000	35/hr.
West	$ 135,000	95,000	85,000	50/hr.

1.2 Average salaries for financial support staff (without benefits)

CFO or director of finance) are likely to have some sort of part- or full-time support staff to handle data entry. A large firm will have an entire finance department, with different people filling specialized roles.

The previously discussed guidelines regarding the size of a firm and when you need to hire for each position are not written in stone, of course. If you, as your firm's principal, have fairly good business sense and savvy, you could have a rock-star bookkeeper who could keep things running, and running well, long after you employ more than twenty people. On the flip side, you may find you want someone with the strategic mind-set of a director of finance, even if you have a staff of just fifteen. It's best to find people who not only can complement your skill set and work style, but also can leverage their business knowledge and expertise to compensate for your shortcomings and allow you to build a better and bigger business, all in the support of your creativity. **FIG 1.2**

BUT REMEMBER: IT'S STILL YOUR MONEY.

Regardless of the strength of your financial team, at the end of the day, you'll be the one held accountable because it is *your* money—and your *clients'* money—and *you* need to understand where it's going. You can hire people to handle the grunt work and even much of the big-picture strategy and systems, but you can never truly delegate the major money decisions. They're all yours. So you have to stay highly attuned to the financial performance of your practice.

The biggest mistake you can make is to absolve yourself of all financial responsibility and give someone else complete control. Unfortunately, it's not unusual for principals who don't care about the money side of their business to hire the wrong person to run it. Given free rein, that person may make mistakes without the principal's knowledge or, even worse, may take advantage. I can't tell you the number of offices I've walked into where bookkeepers have been caught stealing or the controller's paperwork is a mess or the accounts receivable person hasn't been sending out invoices. (For advice on how to avoid personnel mistakes like these, see Chapter Five, "The People You *Don't* Need in Your Life.") And it's not until the firm's principals find themselves in deep financial trouble that they realize something must be wrong.

Regardless of how much you hate looking at your numbers, it's vital that you remain aware of what's going on financially. This means having your staff produce reports that present a limited number of key figures in a way that is clear and easy for you to read—*not* giving you spreadsheet after spreadsheet that will make your eyes glaze over. You must then review these reports, with the help of your finance team, on a monthly basis, taking a deep dive to analyze them once a quarter. Later in this chapter I'll get more into the specifics of these reports, the schedule for looking at them, and the questions you should ask about them.

YOUR FINANCE TEAM AND YOUR CONTRACTS

Your financial support person or people should be in control of your agreements. To do so, they need to know your contract and your contracting systems and processes backward and forward. If you have a controller or a CFO, that person might even handle contract negotiations for you. When you delegate that responsibility, you should be especially clear on what and how much you are willing to negotiate, whether it be related to fees or basic terms. Putting someone else in charge of discussing your agreements with clients saves you from having to do so yourself, which you may appreciate if you don't like conflict. It gives you the opportunity to play "good cop" to your CFO or controller's "bad cop," which can be very helpful. (See Chapter Two, "The Negotiator," for more on this.)

Regardless of who does your negotiating, your contracts should be well vetted by someone with expertise, to ensure that they truly protect both you and your firm. They should not be overly burdensome for your clients; a long and onerous agreement can cause you to lose clients. Most important, your contract's purpose is to clarify all expectations for both parties, laying out what you will do for your clients and what you can expect from them in return. This will minimize changes and debate during the project.

Setting Financial Goals and Budgets

This is the real crux of this chapter—and the heart of your firm's well-being.

At a design firm, setting financial goals is as much about having a crystal ball as it is about knowing and understanding your revenue and expenses. No one ever knows exactly what projects will come in and when—in a given month, let alone in an entire year. The key to setting financial goals and budgets is using what you do know—about your firm, about who you are and how you operate, and about the current business environment—to minimize your reliance on crystal ball–style predictions.

SETTING FINANCIAL GOALS

You can't set financial goals in a vacuum, separate from your budgeting, as that could easily result in your pursuing profit margins that may be unrealistic given your income and expenditures, your fee structure, and your overhead. But you can do some big-picture thinking about the kind of firm you have and want to have and the sort of work you do and want to do. You can then determine the level of pure profit you want to realize.

I've found that 25 percent profitability is a good target number for successful design practices. That 25 percent is based on fees you earn from either your time or the markup you make on purchasing; it is not based on total income, where your purchasing dollars run through your business. This percentage allows firms to charge appropriate fees and take on the right quantity of work for their number of employees, all while covering fixed expenses, as well as discretionary ones, such as marketing and creative projects that can bring in new business. This figure also lets you maintain a reserve for any extraordinary costs that arise.

Extremes do exist outside of this profit margin. Some firms have principals with the philosophy that they need, or want, to be lean and mean to pull in as much profit as possible. They're out to push well past that 25 percent, with the lowest overhead expenditures they can manage plus a wealth of high-paying projects that a small, and ideally cheap, staff completes while working at a white-knuckle pace. This could work, but these firms run the risk of alienating clients, who are likely getting short shrift, and of burning out their staff or even their principals, who are being overworked. They could also be shooting for high profit by charging unreasonably high fees, and that, too, could backfire if they start to lose projects by coming in with bids that are higher than their colleagues' or by adding additional fees after their initial proposals.

Another sort of firm, meanwhile, may decide it wants its studio to be as easygoing, low-key, and creative a work space as fiscally possible—a place where employees feel that they can explore and take their time. They're fine pulling in, say, just a 10 percent profit, due to some combination of high salaries, high overhead expenses, and few or creative projects that don't necessarily produce returns on their investment. This may all be by choice, but if any or all of this just starts happening without a conscious decision, it could mean the firm isn't working efficiently or enough, or that it's not billing what it should, or that its expenses are simply too high. Whether intentional or not, working with a 10 percent profit margin doesn't provide much of a financial cushion in case of emergencies or unusual situations.

And so, I reiterate, you should be shooting for a profit of 25 percent.

Now, how to make that happen? That's where budgeting comes in.

BUDGETING

There are two kinds of budgeting that design firms will typically do: **annual budgeting**, in which a firm plans income and expenditures across an entire year, and **project budgeting**, which plans the same for an individual commission. (This chapter concerns itself largely with annual budgets; for project budgets, please see the project management chapter of my first book, *The Business of Design*.)

Annual Budgeting

Start budgeting for a year with your known, fixed expenses and anticipated variable ones, as well as your revenue projections. As many of these numbers as possible should be known, fixed quantities; when they're not, they should be derived from historical data, accounting for the growth (or contraction) of your business and of the broader economy. You can further budget in any extraordinary expenses you are considering to invest in the growth and development of your firm, all with an eye on your profitability target.

Your Expenses, Fixed and Variable

I had a meeting with a potential client recently in which we reviewed his finances for the previous twelve months. At one point, he turned to me and said, "We made a lot of money—where is it?"

Running a business is expensive, and if you don't plan ahead and strategize—that is, if you don't budget—you may be left wondering where all the money you're pulling in is going. Sometimes, a lag in the collection of your fees combined with a variety of fixed expenses up front simply makes it *look* as though you've got a negative cash flow. But at other times, you may have a more serious problem. Either way, knowing in advance what your expenses are will help.

Here are the major expenses that a design practice should expect:

- **Salaries** Since most creative practices don't sell widgets, but rather sell their time, a firm's labor expenses tend to be its single largest line item. Your firm's labor costs typically will be 33 percent of your income. (All percentages are calculated through dividing the cost by your total income).

- **Rent** Keeping a roof over your firm should typically cost between 2.5 percent and 5 percent of your income, depending on your location. (In some large and expensive cities, such as New York, the rent can be as high as 10 percent of income.)

- **General office expenses** This includes everything from minor desk supplies to major expenditures, such as computer stations and software suites. There was a time when an architect could open a practice by getting a couple of sawhorses, an old door, and a Mayline drafting rule and just starting to draw. Today, however, we're talking about $7,000 on machines and probably another $5,000 to $6,000 for software for every station that you build—a big investment.

- **Benefits** Health insurance and other benefits (life insurance; 401(k) contributions; and holiday, vacation, and sick time) usually should not exceed 25 percent of your line item for salaries. You must decide whether you are covering all of your employees' monthly health-care premiums or just a portion of them. I find that about half of all design firms cover 100 percent of their employees' medical premiums and the other half ask their employees to contribute between 5 and 20 percent of the costs. (Either way, a complete and generous benefits package is a carrot you can offer to hire the best people, so you want it to be as rich as you can afford.)

- **Insurance**   This includes general liability, auto, and professional liability insurance, and it should not exceed 2 percent of your income. Be careful to be well covered but not overinsured. The rule of thumb is to make sure you are covered for a one-time major event—a lawsuit, a project failing, a car accident—but not to carry so much insurance that your premiums have a major effect on your profitability. But this is about comfort; some people are simply more comfortable being overinsured.

- **Marketing**   This includes photography, public relations, and other marketing and promotional expenses—the cost of creating a room at a show house, for example. Typically these line items run about 4 percent to 6 percent of your income.

- **Exploratory creative projects**   A firm will sometimes take on, or even seek out, projects that allow it to expand into a new practice area or move forward in some other way, even though these may end up costing rather than earning money. While the immediate benefit may not be a positive cash flow, the long-term return on investment can be huge. If you have it in mind to pursue some of these loss-leader projects, then you should budget them in. I recommend that you limit your exposure to one or two of these projects per year, tops.

Beyond these line items, which are known as **operating expenses**, you'll also have **reimbursable expenses**—purchases you make on behalf of clients, say, or travel you undertake for a project, both of which your clients will pay you back for—and **direct expenses**, which are not reimbursable but are included in your fees, such as a consultant's services on a project.

Generating Your Revenue Projections

It's long been my belief—and I learned this from Art Gensler, during my days at his firm—that the right way to run a firm is to hire good people first and *then* look for good projects that are right for those people.

Many designers do the reverse, bringing in projects and then hiring people to work on them, but that turns your practice into a hire-fire firm, staffing up when a commission comes in and then laying designers off when the work finishes. And that doesn't create much in the way of loyalty or stability. It can also make budgeting particularly difficult. No firm ever really knows what projects will come in or exactly when and what they will pay. (Again, this would require a crystal ball.) But a hire-fire firm has it doubly bad, because staff size at any point is also unknown, so it is impossible to accurately estimate salary and benefit expenditures over the course of a year.

If you operate as I'm recommending—hiring a great team and then finding the projects that fit that team—you will have a far more successful practice, one filled with like-minded people who fit your firm's ethos and aesthetic. If you don't need to suddenly staff up, you'll have more time when you do need to fill positions, and taking your time hiring is important. Projects may come and go, but employees don't, or at least they shouldn't. If you create a safe and stable environment, bringing in projects tailored to your team, those very good, like-minded, carefully selected people will stick around.

Working this way has the added benefit of making it relatively easy to figure out your income needs, because your revenue goals can be based on staffing numbers and the salaries you need to support that staff.

EMPLOYEE	BILLING RATE	UTILIZATION	HOURS	POTENTIAL BILLING	COST RATE	MULTIPLIER: 3.5	MULTIPLIER: 3.2
Principal	$ 350	45 %	1,824	$ 287,280	$ 120.19	$ 345,288	$ 315,692
Principal	350	50	1,824	319,200	120.19	383,654	350,769
Senior Project Manager	250	75	1,824	342,000	96.15	460,385	420,923
Senior Project Manager	250	75	1,864	349,500	96.15	470,462	430,137
Senior Project Manager	250	80	1,864	372,800	84.13	439,115	401,477
Senior Designer	225	75	1,904	321,300	79.33	396,476	362,492
Senior Designer	225	80	1,904	342,720	79.33	422,924	386,673
Senior Designer	225	80	1,904	342,720	72.12	384,462	351,508
Project Manager	195	80	1,904	297,024	72.12	384,486	351,530
Project Manager	195	85	1,904	315,588	70.00	396,508	362,522
Project Manager	195	85	1,904	315,588	55.29	313,176	286,332
Project Manager	195	85	1,904	315,588	52.88	299,560	273,883
Job Captain	170	90	1,904	291,312	43.27	259,512	237,268
Job Captain	170	90	1,904	291,312	43.27	259,516	237,272
Job Captain	170	90	1,904	291,312	40.87	245,094	224,086
Job Captain	170	90	1,904	291,312	40.87	245,122	224,111
Draftsperson	150	90	1,904	257,040	36.06	216,260	197,723
Draftsperson	150	90	1,904	257,040	36.06	216,273	197,736
Draftsperson	135	95	1,904	244,188	33.65	213,056	194,794
Draftsperson	135	95	1,904	244,188	33.65	213,031	194,772
Draftsperson	135	95	1,904	244,188	33.65	213,031	194,772
Draftsperson	135	95	1,904	244,188	33.65	213,031	194,772
Administration	100	25	1,904	47,600	36.06	60,072	54,923
Administration	100	10	1,904	19,040	31.25	20,825	19,040
Administration	100	5	1,904	9,520	24.04	8,010	7,323
Total Projected Billing				$ 6,653,548		$ 7,079,329	$ 6,472,530

1.3 Sample annual income projection by employee

For firms that know their staff size, we've worked out a formula to calculate annual total revenue goals as a simple multiple of the combined salaries of employees; that number directly relates to the amount of money needed to sustain the staff at its current size. Multiplying the total of your firm's direct salaries (anticipated billable hours times the raw salary cost) by 3.5 will give you the income that will cover the fixed operating expenses listed above and still leave that desired 25 percent profit margin. This shows how much work you will need to pursue over the course of the year, taking into account the fees you set for your projects (see section on fees on page 31). **FIG 1.3**

Of course, the 3.5 multiple isn't hard and fast. The revenue projection needs to cover your expenses and earn you the desired profit, but it shouldn't require you to take on an amount of work that's greater than you can handle. If these numbers don't line up—that is, if this projected revenue based on the salary multiple doesn't cover your expenses and allow for the 25 percent profit margin—you probably will need to make some adjustments. It may be that your salaries are too high or that you're overstaffed or that your billing rates don't accommodate the cost of your salaries, meaning that you need to raise your rates (I often find that designers forget to raise their billing rates as they give their staff raises, cutting into their profit margin). It can also mean that your fixed overhead is too high or you're allocating too much for flexible overhead expenses, such as marketing and loss-leader design projects. You'll need to make changes accordingly.

The Importance of Annual Budgeting

Keep in mind that budgeting is all about planning ahead, which is why it happens in anticipation of the year to come. Beyond establishing your expected income and expenses, the process creates stability in your office and a strategy for the next twelve months. Budgeting makes you consider how big your staff is, how large your expenses are, and how much work you already have on your plate, and it helps you to determine how much more work you may need to go after and how many people you would have to hire. It sets expectations and minimizes surprises. To make a driving analogy, your budget helps you look at the road ahead of you and not just the car in front of you.

If you're budgeting, and therefore planning, you can anticipate different scenarios and model different outcomes for how your practice will function in the months and years ahead. Being ready for the possibility that a major client will slip away or that a project will be put on hold leaves you less vulnerable and more nimble. (For more on what to do in situations like these, see the section on troubleshooting at the end of this chapter.)

Because the budgeting process is really about ensuring stability throughout the year, you shouldn't adjust it more than once in a twelve-month period unless something really drastic happens. If a huge project goes away or something massive comes in, you can, and should, make changes. But if you're adjusting your numbers on a regular basis, you're not budgeting; you're just tracking. And that undercuts one of the major benefits of budgeting, which is the ability to look back throughout (and at the end of) the year, to compare your projections with how you're doing. A budget has importance as a backward-looking tool that is as vital as its forward-looking value.

The Importance of Budgeting for Individual Projects

The importance of budgeting doesn't just apply to your overall financial success but also to the success of individual projects. You want to set out in advance how much time the members of your staff will have to work on a project, based on fees as well as anticipated expenses, and to look at these in relation to the projected revenue. (See opposite for how to establish fees.) Sharing a clear project budget with your team helps that team succeed. It helps them understand the financial situation and establishes expectations. If they come in every day to work on a project with no idea they're working against a fee, let alone what that fee is, there's a good chance they—and you—will wake up one day and find there's no money left to finish the project.

Setting (and Sticking to) Your Fees

There are several different ways that design firms can structure their fees, all of which are discussed in Chapter Two of my first book. Here, suffice it to say that one of the most common practices for architects and designers is to base a project's fee on a percentage of the total cost of construction, or, in the case of interior decorators, the furnishing budget. So, if an architect is commissioned to design a house that will cost $3 million to build, and the firm set its fees at 15 percent of construction costs, the architect would be paid $450,000.

A fee of 15 percent of construction costs for residential work is generally appropriate for the majority of firms in most of the country, but I do see a range from 10 to 25 percent, depending on where the firm is, its client base, and its recognition in the industry and in the public consciousness. On page 32 is a look at ranges for various regions of the United States. **FIG 1.4**

The fee structure you establish should remain fixed, as it directly relates to the value that you and your work have in the marketplace. I'll go over in greater detail why it is vital that you remain steadfast in your fee structure in Chapter Two, "The Negotiator," where I'll also explain how to do so. For now, I'll just note that firmly established fees help you create the most rational financial goals, budgets, and revenue projections, both for the year and for individual projects. Allowing those fees to be flexible seriously compromises the accuracy of your projections and can make it very hard for you to conduct business successfully.

In addition to calculating fees as a percentage of some number, many of our clients mark up their reimbursable expenses by 10 to 20 percent. The markup covers the costs of using your funds in advance and the administration costs of managing and billing these expenses.

INTERIOR DESIGN

FEE TYPE	Northeast	Southeast	Midwest	South	West
Hourly [1]	$ 100–300	75–250	75–250	75–250	100–250
% of Purchases	30–35 %	25–30	25–30	25–30	30–35
Per square foot [2]	$ 20	10	10	10	15
Lump sum [3]	(Based on numbers above but locked in from beginning)				

1. Range from junior designer to principal
2. Design fee plus markup
3. Usually based on lump-sum fee plus markup

ARCHITECTURE

FEE TYPE	Northeast	Southeast	Midwest	South	West
Hourly [4]	$ 100–350	75–250	75–250	75–200	100–300
% of Construction	15–18 %	8–10	8–12	8–12	15–18
Per square foot [5]	$ 100	75	75	65	90
Lump sum [6]	(Based on numbers above but locked in from beginning)				

4. Range from draftsperson to principal
5. Adjusted as project increases in size
6. Based on percentage but is not adjusted as project increases in cost

1.4   Fee structures by region. These are average fee structures for interior design and architecture, but individuals in any creative field can use these numbers to determine fees.

A Note on Billing and Cash Flow

Designers who are just starting to build their firms and hire their first employees may not realize that there can be significant—and financially challenging—lag time between the work that a firm does and when it gets paid. When you're a solo practitioner, this can be frustrating, but once you have a staff to provide for, it can become more than just frustrating.

You're paying your employees as they do their work for you, generally in the middle and at the end of the month. Your clients, however, are probably only paying you monthly, at best, and you can only bill them for work that you and your staff have already done. And *then* they may not pay you for thirty, forty-five, or even sixty days *after* you've billed them. In that time you will have gone through as many as four pay periods for your employees.

The first thing to realize is that you will need a chunk of capital, some cash on hand, before you add staff; the second thing is the importance of billing in a timely manner—and then following up and collecting on those billings.

If you have the systems in place to get your billings out by the first or second week of every month and then have someone who can help you chase down

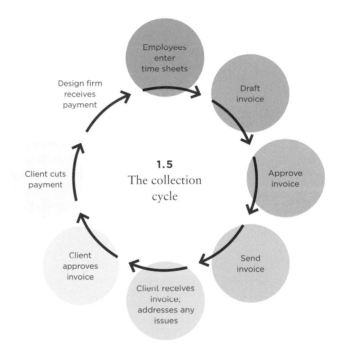

1.5
The collection cycle

Employees enter time sheets

Draft invoice

Approve invoice

Send invoice

Client receives invoice; addresses any issues

Client approves invoice

Client cuts payment

Design firm receives payment

payment, then you are likely to see income for those invoices in closer to thirty than sixty days. Even then, though, you're looking at two payment cycles before the funds from a client come in, so you need to have enough overall cash flow—that is, funds coming in from the (timely, efficient) invoices of prior months—to cover the costs of your staff and other overhead expenses. **FIG 1.5**

Reports That You Can Understand

The best way to remain fully aware of your firm's financial performance is to have your finance team produce reports that are easy for you to read. These should be presented to you at regular intervals, and you should go over them with your financier or financiers. This could take as little as an hour and up to two or three hours in more challenging times.

Here's a look at the reports that you should see on a weekly, monthly, and quarterly basis:

- **Income statement** Also called a P&L statement, this document compares monthly income and expenses for the current month and year to date. It quickly highlights any issues in your revenue and expenses. *You should review monthly.*

- **Balance sheet** A report that shows you your assets, liabilities, and net worth. This is where you can see your cash position and your accounts receivable and accounts payable obligations. *You should review monthly.*

- **Profit planning report** Also known as an operational budget report or an actual-versus-budget analysis. It compares the actual income and expenses from your income statement with the expected numbers from your annual budget. It is a great tool because it illustrates how you're matching your projected forecasts. *You should review monthly.*

- **General ledger** A data report that details each individual income and expense by category. For example, if you are looking at the general ledger for marketing, you could see costs for advertising or a PR consultant or lunch with a client. *Your* *financial person should review this monthly and report any extraordinary expenses in summary form to you.*

- **Purchasing report** A report showing you the status of all your firm's purchasing activities: how much vendors need to be paid, how much the client has paid you for items, and what remains to be paid. *You should review weekly.*

- **Accounts receivable report** This tracks who owes your firm money, how much, when they were billed, and when they are (or were) expected to pay you. It's helpful because it quickly reveals how much money your firm is owed and who your problem payers are. *You should review weekly.*

- **Accounts payable report** The flip side of the accounts receivable report, this statement shows who your firm owes money *to,* how much, and when it is (or was) due. *You should review weekly.*

You should look at most reports on a weekly or monthly basis, and it's important to analyze your financial position once a quarter. That means diving in and seeing how well you're doing compared to budget and revenue projections. An executive summary is a table and dashboard that we've created and tweaked over the years at Granet & Associates to give highly creative people an easy-to-read look at their top-line numbers. It places all the key financial information on a single one-page document. You can look at the current month, the previous month, and the year to date and compare each number with its budgeted correlatives. This immediately and easily makes clear how well (or poorly) the firm is doing vis-à-vis expectations. **FIGS 1.6 + 1.7**

None of these frequencies are written in stone. When you're first starting your business, you should know what your cash flow is on a weekly basis, so you should

Executive Summary

Redwood
Design Group

	Current Period Actual	Current Period Budget	Year to Date Actual	Year to Date Budget	Prior Period Actual
INCOME-RELATED DATA					
Total Income	$ 225,000	240,000	474,000	480,000	249,000
Reimbursable Inc. Less Expenses	$ 2,200	2,500	4,800	5,000	2,600
Direct Project Expenses	$ 24,000	20,000	42,000	40,000	18,000
Overhead Expenses	$ 82,678	90,000	174,134	180,000	91,456
Net Profit	$ 41,110	49,000	103,442	98,000	62,332
Overhead	1.38 %	1.38	1.45	1.38	1.52
Break-Even	2.38 %	2.38	2.45	2.38	2.52
LABOR-RELATED DATA					
Total Net Fees	$ 201,000	220,000	432,000	440,000	231,000
Direct Labor	$ 60,000	65,000	120,000	130,000	60,000
Indirect Labor	$ 17,212	16,000	34,424	32,000	17,212
Total Salaries	$ 77,212	81,000	154,424	162,000	77,212
Effective Multiplier	3.35	3.38	3.60	3.38	3.85
Staff Utilization	76.00 %	75.00	77.00	74.00	78.00

OTHER FINANCIAL DATA	This Month	Last Month
Checking Account Balance	$ 28,222	12,333
Savings Account Balance	$ 90,000	90,000
Retainer Account	$ 8,894	8,894
Line of Credit Outstanding	$ 50,000	25,000
Accounts Payable	$ 9,200	0
Accounts Receivable	$ 612,500	518,000

1.6   Sample monthly executive summary

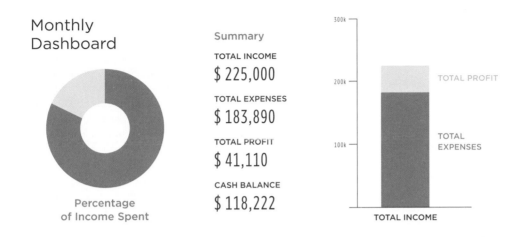

Monthly Dashboard

Percentage of Income Spent

Summary

TOTAL INCOME
$ 225,000

TOTAL EXPENSES
$ 183,890

TOTAL PROFIT
$ 41,110

CASH BALANCE
$ 118,222

TOTAL PROFIT

TOTAL EXPENSES

TOTAL INCOME

300k

200k

100k

1.7 Sample monthly executive summary dashboard

look at your accounts receivable and payable every week. As you become more stable, you could look at it on a monthly basis. Similarly, when things are stable, you can look at the executive summary quarterly, but should there be issues, you should go over it monthly.

The frequency with which you need to see data and really analyze it ties directly into how good your cash flow is and how successfully your projects and your business are running. You always need to review the numbers, but good times generally require less strategic management and allocation of funds.

During bad economic times you may need to analyze your finances every month, not just once a quarter. There may not be a lot you can do from month to month to make a change quickly, but doing the deep-dive analysis frequently will make it clear if things are taking a turn, and that will allow you to start planning for change sooner. There were times in 2009—when everything was falling apart in the depths of the recession—when people were looking at their finances daily to see how much money they had in the bank, figuring out how they were going to bill, how to collect, and how to pay vendors and staff.

Regardless of how frequently you review and analyze these statements, you shouldn't be a passive observer when going over these reports with your finance team. Some key questions are:

- How is our cash flow, and do you see any issues or concerns with our meeting the financial obligations of the next month?

- Who is more than sixty days late paying us?

- Do we have any unsigned agreements outstanding?

- What projects are on our proposal list? How real are they?

- Are there any expenses that were out of line with our budget this month?

- Do we anticipate any extraordinary expenses in the coming months?

- Are there any retainers we need to either apply or return to clients?

- Are there any projects that have lost money in the month?

- Are there any staff members due for raises?

- Do we have any hiring needs in the near future?

"You have to know when to trust someone to do his or her job—when your focus as a creative person is on the creative side, to let somebody else figure out how to nurture that and how to make it into a long-term business." **MARC SZAFRAN**

Death and Taxes

Benjamin Franklin wrote, "In this world nothing can be said to be certain, except death and taxes." (And he should know. He's on the $100 bill.) This section is much more about taxes than death, though sometimes I think taxes will be the death of me.

I won't discuss how you can get creative at the end of the year, lest the IRS come after me, but there are things you can do to be smart about filing your returns.

When figuring out your year-end tax liability, you should work closely with your accountant to understand the best use of your money. Here are four good year-end financial decisions that can lower your tax burden and are completely within the confines of what's allowable.

- Look into Section 179 deductions. These were instituted to stimulate the economy by allowing companies to take a large amount of their capital expenses and deduct them in one given year rather than depreciating these expenses over many years. Each year the IRS determines how much this deduction will be.

- Plan your year-end expenses to get a tax deduction in the current year. You can reduce your tax burden for a profitable year through strategic purchasing. If cash flow is tight, you can still use lines of credit and credit cards; even though these expenses are not paid in cash, your liability for these expenses is fully deductible in the year you incurred the expense.

- Determine whether you should fund employee retirement plans or provide year-end staff bonuses, both of which you can claim as deductions. Wouldn't you rather give your staff a larger bonus than pay 50 percent of the same dollars to Uncle Sam? You can claim profit-sharing payments as deductions for the current year, but you are not then obligated to pay them out until you actually file your taxes. This gives you the tax benefit of the deduction even if you don't have the immediate cash to pay for it.

- You can slow down your billing to allow clients to pay you at the beginning of the next year rather than at the end of the current one, thereby lowering your earnings and, by extension, your tax burden. If you file your taxes on a cash basis, you are only required to report cash receipts in the year you have deposited them. (Companies that file on an accrual basis report billings, not collected cash receipts.)

Troubleshooting

Even with a great finance team in place, as well as informed budgeting and strong reporting and smart tracking systems, things can—and indeed, will—sometimes take a downward turn. The reason could be anything from a blip in the global economy to an individual client putting a project on hold. Advance planning and a reserve of cash can help you weather these storms. But here's a look at three particularly common challenges and specific strategies to overcome them. ▶

The key to your financial success is to be supported by the right financial people. Figure out whom you need and then figure out what you need from them and communicate on a regular basis. First go for quantity of communication; eventually, when you are in a groove, you will develop a communication shorthand. There is nothing more freeing for your creativity than a solid financial foundation.

> "Work with people who are going to be there when the shit hits the fan, because it always does."
> **CHRIS POLLACK**

IF...	THEN...
A client puts your project on hold or stops it suddenly:	• Determine how you may absorb the staff from this project into other projects.
	• Apply the nonrefundable retainer; this can help with the slowdown until you replace the project.
	• Look at reducing expenses.
	• You may need to consider layoffs.
A client stops paying for an in-process project:	• Decide if you are going to stop work or try to negotiate with the client.
	• Send your client a letter expressing your intention to stop work unless you are paid immediately.
	• Consider what phase the project is in and if you could apply any leverage by holding up designs or drawings.
	• Apply the client's retainer to outstanding balances.
	• If everything else fails, you may have to consider taking legal action.
A project starts to lose money due to your mismanagement, and it's not the fault of the client:	• Meet with your project manager to get a handle on the current state of the project.
	• Analyze how much of the total fee you have used and figure out how much you have left to complete the project.
	• Inform your staff about how much time they can work on the project moving forward, in order to complete the commission without incurring further loss (or, at the very least, to slow that loss).
	• Determine if any of the services you have been offering the client are outside the scope of your original contract and can be billed as additional services.

CHAPTER TWO

The Negotiator: Communicating Value

IF THE FINANCIAL SUBJECTS I covered in the previous chapter can be considered a sort of science, then negotiation is much more of an art, one requiring finesse, strategy, and often a bit of theatricality.

Your fees—that is, your finances—are the end, and negotiating is a means to that end. It's a process of inquiry and advocacy through which you first come to understand a prospective (or repeat) client's needs and then establish (or reestablish) the value of your talent in helping the client meet those needs.

Negotiation's purpose is to ensure that you and your firm are paid what you're worth for the work that you do. And this matters because your success depends upon maintaining the value of your creative talent, not just for any individual client but in the marketplace more broadly.

Negotiating in the design business shouldn't ever be about slashing fees to win a project, or, even worse, to undercut and outbid a colleague, whether to win a project in the first place or to steal it away from someone later. (Remember, a client may

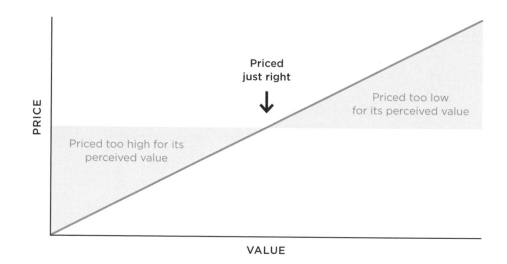

2.1 Price vs. value

be around for just one commission, but your community of colleagues and peers is forever.) Nor is it about squeezing every last penny you can out of a client.

Negotiating is about educating your clients on how you determine your fees and then convincing them that those fees are appropriate by connecting them to the clients' own projects. **FIG 2.1**

Having established fair, appropriate, and financially sustainable fees—based on the guidelines I laid out in the previous chapter—you will need to be firm, unflinching even, in sticking to those numbers.

This chapter, then, isn't really about negotiating your pricing scheme at all but instead about strategies and processes to ensure that you always get your standard fees. I'll explain how to win work without adjusting your rates or your terms ("terms" being everything from collection times to completion schedules and timelines to reimbursable expenses).

When you help clients understand why your fees are what they are, and why they correctly correspond to the value you and your firm provide, you'll never have to negotiate your rates down.

How to Negotiate in the Design Business

When was the last time you went to your doctor or your lawyer or your dentist and negotiated about the fee? Never, right?

You don't do that, because these professions have established precedents for how and what they charge, and people's expectations match that. The services those other professionals provide also have the advantage of being what I think of as necessary evils. In contrast, the services interior designers and, to some extent, architects provide are often seen by the public as luxuries. But ask anyone who's ever had a do-it-yourself building, renovation, or decoration project go horribly awry whether he thinks hiring a designer is a luxury. Chances are, he now knows the amount he would have paid a designer could have saved him the thousands and thousands he sunk into his failed DIY project. And yet, we designers can have a difficult time convincing clients of the value of our talent and skill, and that makes it very difficult to advocate for our established fees and pricing structure.

In part, this difficulty is a matter of public perception. There's an idea out there that designers add tremendous markups to materials, products, furnishings, labor, and even reimbursable expenses, asking our clients to pay exorbitant rates above actual cost. My response to this is always to draw an analogy to retail: you don't go to Nordstrom and expect to pay the same price for a pair of shoes that the store's wholesale buyers pay; the retailer gets a rate based on volume, the same way we do as designers, and then the store marks up the price, both to cover the cost of its overhead—rent, staffing, et cetera—and to make a profit.

No one expects to have access to a Nordstrom shoe buyer's pricing structure, and no one expects a dentist to cut her rates, nor does anyone think these folks shouldn't make a profit. It's our job, then, when advocating for our services, to educate clients so they understand that (a) hiring us is necessary, (b) our rates are fixed and based on the very real value we provide, and (c) these rates earn us an appropriate profit after our overhead is taken out.

The question, of course, is how to make clients understand all this—how to make the process about fee education rather than rate negotiation.

SEVEN STRATEGIES FOR SUCCESSFUL NEGOTIATION
1. Be confident.

When someone is trying to negotiate with you, your value and the value of your talent are under attack. You need to protect those things, and to do that, you need to be confident and to project confidence, standing firm in the belief that clients need you, that you can give them what they are looking for, and that your fees are entirely apt. The more confident you are about your talent and its value, the less you should actually have to negotiate, even if a prospective client's negotiating skills outmatch yours.

Not long ago, one of my clients was having a meeting to discuss a potential project with a major real estate developer. The developer's office featured a chain saw attached to a plaque that said something like: "Congratulations for cutting fees and costs to get this building built." My client stared at that award, dumbstruck. And then he started talking about negotiating his fees. "Clearly I'm not going to win," he said, gesturing at the chain saw. "And, quite honestly, maybe I'm not the right fit for you. I know you like my work, but you know my costs, and you know my fees don't earn me millions of dollars on every project. They're fair and honest, and they are what they are."

With those few sentences, my client tipped his hat to the developer's negotiating skills and appealed to his ego. Doing so defused the entire situation, and my client walked out with the fees he wanted. The moral of the story is: Even if you're outgunned—or, in this case, outchainsawed—never let them smell fear. Never let them think they can negotiate.

2. Operate from a position of strength.

As you become more well known and admired for your work, you'll find you have to negotiate less and less, as your reputation—and your value—will precede you. But even the most talented and sought-after designers may find themselves negotiating when they want to win a project they really covet. This is dangerous, however, as it gives the client the upper hand. Even if you really want a project, you still need to remain in the driver's seat.

Here's an example of something one of my clients, a talented and in-demand Los Angeles designer, does when meeting with a prospective client. Before the meeting is over he will ask, "What other designers are you talking with?" Even if the answer is, "We're only talking to you; you're the one we want," his approach is, "You should look around. Here are three names; go meet them."

Designers think this is risky; they worry they'll lose a client. But nine times out of ten, that client will return to you—probably without even having talked to anyone else. Clients want you more if you seem like you're not all that interested. It's the old playing-hard-to-get trick. It suggests that you're operating not from fear but from strength, the strength to say, "No, please, go look around; make sure I'm the person for you," and that you have the confidence to know they'll come back. (And if the prospective clients *do* end up going with a colleague you recommend, they probably weren't right for you anyway.)

3. Listen to the client.

Get into the other person's head to find out what she wants. I'll discuss this further, under "Inquiry and Advocacy," but it's also worth noting as a strategy: in order to negotiate, you have to understand the prospective client's desires and goals, as well as her concerns and fears.

A client once asked me to sit in and observe a meeting with a potential client. Halfway through the meeting, I noticed that his client, a well-known actress, was getting restless, and she soon excused herself to use the restroom. Once she was out of earshot, I turned to my client and said, "You are not listening to her. She has said four times that she wants this project to be fun, and you've made it all sound like logistics." He responded that he'd never heard her say that. (Like I said, he wasn't listening!) When she returned to the meeting, the first words out of his mouth were, "I hope you know that once we deal with all the little contract details, this is going to be a really fun process." The actress slammed her hand down on the table and said, "Finally! I was waiting for you to say that—I really do want to have fun with this." The result? My client got the commission and the fees he wanted.

As much as you can entice clients to work with you by discussing your background and your ideas for a project, you also have to tailor your talking points to your clients' needs and desires. This builds a convincing case for the value your talent has for them specifically, and they'll be that much more willing to pay for it.

4. Be fair.

With understanding should come fairness, the ability to see that something may not be quite right in a proposal and that a client may have a valid point or concern. For example, sometimes buildings have engineering or code requirements that add tremendously to a project's budget but may have nothing to do with a designer or a design scheme. You should not include these in your fees.

5. Articulate your value.

Of course, it isn't all about the client, and you will want to talk about your past projects and successes. But do that in the context of your prospective clients' project, to help them understand what you can do for them and why that will cost what it does. Take them on tours of different completed projects you've done—ideally in person or, if need be, through photos—explaining why each had its own cost per square foot, so they understand what their money gets them; present examples of budgets, timelines, and team structures your office has created for past commissions, so they see the organizational acumen you bring to the table. I'll talk more about these tactics in greater detail in the "Inquiry and Advocacy" section later in this chapter.

6. Allay fears.

Clients bring all sorts of concerns to the table. It's your job to draw these out—see "Listen to the client," opposite, and "Inquiry and Advocacy," on page 57—and then make clients understand that you're there for them, that you're on their side and will not take advantage of them.

People often think that an architect or designer is going to push them into buying something expensive or spending some amount of money that they're not comfortable with. You should remind them that they can always say no—every decision is truly the client's own.

7. Be flexible.

A willingness to make adjustments—in scheduling, in materials, in staffing, but not in rates or fees—will allow you and the client to arrive at a signed contract.

Clients can get caught up in thinking that our primary motivation as designers is to make money. But, in fact, we're here to be the agent for our clients, to give them the best project within their budget. We have to explain that to clients and make sure that they don't lose sight of that.

THE POWER OF TRUST

All these strategies boil down to one thing: establishing trust. The more people trust you, the more apt they are to accept your fees. They believe in what you're doing for them and what your services are, and they understand that you're being honest in what you're charging them.

Building trust takes time, and you probably don't have a lot of time at the beginning of your relationship with a prospective client. So the question becomes: How do you establish trust quickly with someone you're hoping to work with?

The answer comes down to getting all the details—all the little things a client requires—correct from the very beginning. This means short response times to emails and phone calls, showing up on time to appointments, being prepared for meetings, providing good answers to questions, and being available, within reason, in these early stages. Stay on the ball with all of these elements, and you're well on your way to establishing long-term trust with a new client.

Imagine your relationship with a client as a bank account. Throughout the process of working together, you are constantly making deposits of trust into that account. Eventually, you build up quite a lot of trust savings. At that point, if you make a mistake, some trust may come out of the account, but the effect on the total will be relatively small because you've kept a high balance. In contrast, if your account is low on trust and you make a mistake, there will be very little reserve to draw upon, and your relationship with the client could end.

Trust is a two-way street; you also should notice how a prospective client treats you and your staff, right from the beginning. If he or she is unresponsive or, even worse, abusive during these early phases, don't expect that to change; it will only get worse. If you and your team aren't being treated well, you need to seriously assess whether you want this person as a client.

WHEN NEGOTIATING HAPPENS

I'm a big believer in getting all fees, terms, and conditions squared away at the beginning of the process, before a project begins, through creating and signing a contract with clients. If you do things piecemeal or are at all wishy-washy about your approach to fees, the client is likely to take advantage of that. Delaying settling the details of your agreement sets you up for acrimony later and makes it likely that you'll find yourself doing more than you intended to, and for less money. I have never known anyone who could successfully negotiate in the middle of a project; as a project moves forward, it only becomes harder to agree on terms.

Basic contracts often don't cover certain areas; you should add these points to your agreements:

- A statement that you own your designs and any other intellectual property you bring to the client. These are your original ideas and should not be given away.

- Complete and detailed clarification of the size, scope, and time-line of the project. Without this clarification projects can drag on, and before you know it, your fees will dry up.

- A guarantee that you may raise your rates on an annual basis. One issue that designers often do not address is that every cost of a business—including salaries and other staff costs—will increase annually. Therefore, you need to be able to increase your billing rates, or your margins will drop and your profit will suffer. If you base your billing on a certain percentage of total construction costs—which is a very common and highly successful way to structure fees (see the section on fees in Chapter One)—you need to make sure your contract has language guaranteeing that your total fee (though not the percentage) will go up should construction costs increase.

- The ability to photograph your work. It's important for you to be able to document and ultimately publish your work for marketing purposes. Some particularly private clients may take issue with the "publish" portion of that, but at the very least, you need to have images for your portfolio. Clients who don't want their home in magazines may not have a problem with it being in a book, such as your monograph; you may be able to get them to agree to magazine publication if they remain entirely anonymous.

- Limited liability. Whenever possible, try to include language that allows you to limit your liability to the amount of your fees, no matter what the claim is. (This often is not an easy clause to convince a client to agree to.)

- Language stating that you will receive a termination fee if a project is put on hold and the client doesn't move forward. This fee covers the revenue you would lose while you try to replace the project; it takes time and effort to bring in a new project, to move staff from one project to another, and to begin billing. This clause is essential if you have committed a tremendous amount of your resources to one project.

- For interior designers and decorators, a clause that removes your liability for authenticating antiques you buy on behalf of your clients. This clause ensures that the dealer, not you, will be held accountable if a particular item is not what the dealer represented to you.

Most designers are born without the conflict gene, and so they often avoid talking about fees and terms and contracts. This approach will come back to haunt you, however. You and the client need to create a formal contract and sign on the dotted line. A simple handshake agreement opens up the potential for too many problems—not least of which are liability and lawsuits—that will create trouble for you if you need to get out of a project that you never should have started in the first place.

The truth is, however, that trust is more important than a contract because trust builds a real relationship, whereas a contract can ultimately be meaningless. At the end of the day, if you ever have a disagreement with a wealthy client who comes at you with legal action, you may not have the financial resources to win, even if you're in the right as far as your contract is concerned.

WHOM YOU NEGOTIATE WITH

For the most part, designers negotiate with **potential clients**—and that's what most of this chapter is about—but you also will find yourself in negotiations with **members of your staff**, both new and established, and with **colleagues, collaborators, and vendors**.

My philosophy is to pay staff more rather than less, because you get what you pay for. But that isn't everyone's approach. I had a client who used to say to me, "Here's how I hire talented people: I get them into the office, I get them excited about my work, and then, if I'm really interested in them and I know they're interested in me,

I say, 'I want to hire you but I'm worried I can't afford you.'" This would force the potential hire to be less aggressive in the request, and my client would use her claim of poverty to further negotiate with the recruit.

But you're starting off on the wrong foot when you operate that way. To my mind, if someone asks for $50,000, you should give that person $55,000. Not only does it show that you believe in the person's talent, it also tends to make the staffer work harder every day to prove that he's worth every extra penny. If an employee starts off feeling as if he's worth more than you're paying him, he may end up cutting corners as a result. Start people off on a high note, feeling as though you have seen something in them and are willing to pay for it.

I'll admit that there have been instances when I've offered new hires more than they asked for and they've proven me totally wrong, turning out to be worth maybe only half of what I'd decided to pay them. But 90 percent of the time, this has been the right approach. (When it's not, I don't let the staff member stick around for long; see Chapter Four, "Building the Right Team.")

People often tie their worth to their job title and maybe even use that title in their negotiations when interviewing for a new job. But keep in mind that a project manager at one firm may not be a project manager at another, simply because the size and scope of projects differ so much among firms. It's always been my feeling that a title follows you through a project; it's not a crown you wear all day long. So for one commission, a member of your staff may be a project manager, for another a job captain, and for another a draftsperson.

Dealing with colleagues, collaborators, and vendors is less about negotiating and more about getting fair—or maybe even special—value and top-quality work from people based on how you treat them. How you treat vendors is how they will treat you. If you use an upholsterer who's in high demand and you pay on time, make quick decisions, and are respectful of him and his work, then he will make sure your project gets done on time—probably even first—and particularly well, compared to the project of someone who doesn't take as good care of him.

Loyalty plays a role, too. If you use the same structural engineers again and again, you know that they'll give you their best pricing, not just because they know you but because you provide a steady stream of business. But if you're constantly shopping projects around to different subcontractors and vendors, you can't be sure of the caliber of work you'll be getting, and since you'll always be a new client, you're not likely to get the best pricing.

Negotiating with vendors is not all about money—in fact, very little of it is about money.

Defining and Communicating Value to Clients

Negotiating begins and ends with a question: What is your value to a client? To establish this for someone who is considering hiring you, you need to first establish it for yourself, both in general and for the specific potential client.

Generally speaking, we look at *what* we do and *how* we do it to figure out our core competency and unique selling points, and we imagine that this establishes value for our clients. And the "what" and the "how" are, of course, important, but they're actually secondary to the "why." This is something I learned from one of my favorite TED Talks, given by Simon Sinek, an ethnographer and author most famous for his "Start with Why" concept and book. I've summarized his ideas about leadership here, but I encourage everyone to watch his TED presentation.

The great companies, the great leaders, the great innovators, they focus on the "why." As Sinek explains: "People don't buy what you do; they buy *why* you do it.…If you talk about what you believe, you will attract those who believe what you believe."

You need to establish your own "why" and then sell that "why." If you've been selling your "what" or your "how," you want to work to translate that to a "why." Some firms sell a particular aesthetic, for example, and clients come to them and value them for that. Sinek's point is that rather than buying just an aesthetic, people want to buy into your passion for the style and your desire to share it with others because it improves people's lives and makes the world a better place.

This is true of starchitects such as Frank Gehry or Richard Meier; not only do their buildings have a specific look and feel, but each architect has his own specific point of view. Their passion for both, and sharing both, is palpable.

But this isn't just about starchitects. I have a less well-known designer client who specializes in classical architecture. His value to clients is bound up in his mastery of this style (his "what"), but even more so in the "why." His value lies in his unique ability to interpret classicism for his clients and the way they live today, sharing his passion for the aesthetic and the way it improves their enjoyment of where they live, their well-being. People come to him for this, and he knows that.

Other firms pride themselves on an ability to design in multiple styles, multiple languages, multiple vernaculars. They may be selling their ability to understand and interpret these various aesthetics, as well as their capacity for understanding and interpreting the needs and desires of clients. But they'd do even better at establishing their value for clients if they started with "why"—the fact that they love helping people create a home that is uniquely, powerfully their own, assisting clients as they unlock their desires, helping them discover what makes them happy about a space and what style might best match that.

Still other firms may define their value based on the level of service and involvement they provide, especially by the office's principal or principals. Maybe you pride yourself on being a top project manager or on finishing work on time and under budget. Or perhaps you have particular skill in overcoming logistical hurdles. Maybe you're all about being on call for your clients 24/7 and always being in meetings with them. I've had many, many designers tell me that their clients select them because they, as their firm's principal, will be involved in a project. When people hire a designer, they tend to hope that they're going to work directly with that person, so offering that is a major value proposition. In that case, your "why" could be about your love for hands-on, direct involvement with clients from the very beginning of a project to the very end, helping them realize their dream of a perfect home. But there's also value in a team approach, and you could just as legitimately define your worth based on your ability to assemble groups of talented individuals to take on projects of different scopes.

Once you've defined the "why" of your firm's value generally—and it can even be some combination of the three examples above—you need to define it for a specific client's particular project. Winning work may seem like something that's largely about you, but, in fact, it's much more about the client. Based on what you learn from clients and what you ascertain about their needs, you can tailor your services to match their needs. The best clients believe the same things as you, and the most successful firms work with like-minded clients.

INQUIRY AND ADVOCACY

There are two key parts to defining and communicating the value of your "why" and your talent to clients.

The first is **inquiry**: asking the questions—and, just as important, listening to the answers—that help you understand a client's "why." Why she is doing her project and why she is coming to you. Then you can determine what the commission is, what the goals and concerns are, and how the client envisions working on and completing the project.

Are you somebody whose passion, point of view, and work the client admires, someone whose aesthetic matches her own? If so, you have an advantage, in that she already appreciates what you do. Then you can find out what it is about you and your work that resonates with her and use that information as you move forward.

Often, however, clients see designers as commodities (a "what," not a "why"): they need to get something done and they can't do it themselves, so they have to hire *someone*. Maybe it'll be you, but it could just as easily be someone else, especially if someone else's price is lower. In those instances, it's even more important to get a handle on a project's and a client's "why." To sell yourself—your "why," your ideas, and your services—you must first find out whether there's really any affinity for them, and if there is, where that interest comes from.

Seven Key Questions

- Why are you building this project?

- What about this project is important to you?

- Why have you come to us?

- What are some places or spaces that have appealed to you in the past, and why do you think you found them appealing?

- Have you ever done a project like this before?

- Can you tell me about how you live and how you work—and what is significant to you about the way you experience your home and work life?

- What are the three things that you hold near and dear?

Only after you've gotten a full picture of these points can you determine if this is a project and a client that's right for you. If the answer is yes, you can then begin defining and communicating the value of your "why" and your work. You'll create a tailored, specific definition of what your value will be for the client on this commission.

From here, you can turn to the second part: **advocacy**. This means communicating your value by educating the clients on the value of your services—as ever, starting with "why" and then moving on to *what* you do and *how* you do it. You want to impress clients with your passion for what you do and your desire to share it with others (the "why"), and then dazzle them with your skills, both aesthetic and organizational (the "what"), as well as the complete service you provide (the "how"). Throughout, you'll be helping clients understand why things cost what they cost. **FIG 2.2**

INQUIRY (do first)

Learn about your clients.

Explore their likes and dislikes.

Find a connection you have with them.

Find out why they like your work.

Find out how they found out about you.

ADVOCACY (do second)

Tell them why you do what you do.

Share with them your strengths.

Give an example of what you learned about them and why you can service them well.

Begin to show relevant work that your clients can relate to.

Share an idea or two.

2.2 Inquiry and advocacy

Three Advocacy Strategies That Establish Value

Start with why: reveal your passion

Begin by explaining why you're a designer and why you're the kind of designer you are. What's the passion that brought you to this field? How do you share this passion and use it to improve people's lives or even the world? From here, move into why you'd love the opportunity to work with this client on this project. How do you see it lining up with your "why"?

Move on to what: show off your projects

After you've established your "why" for clients, the most important aspect of advocacy is probably sharing your past work. Taking them on a tour of completed commissions that relate to their own project, either through pictures or, even better, live and in person, provides them with the best sense of you and your work and allows you to draw connections between what you've done for others and what you can do for them. This is your "what."

Use these tours as teachable moments. If you can show projects at different price tiers, all the better. That lets clients see what detailing and finishes look like at $400 per square foot compared to $800. It makes these differences very clear for someone who may not otherwise understand and goes a long way toward explaining why you are more expensive than others. What I hear constantly, especially in residential work, is, "My neighbor built a house for $200 a square foot, and your houses are $600, and I don't see why." A house tour is your chance to clarify what can be done that will cost more or less—maybe even addressing the fact that a client's budget may not match what he or she has in mind in terms of program and scope or level of finishes and detailing.

Then get to how: explain your process and procedures
Beyond the house tour, you should also advocate for your worth by giving clients a sense of your process and relating that to your fee structure. This is your "how." If you pride yourself on your involvement in projects, now's the time to explain that you're different from someone who just hands off a set of drawings to a builder. If you like to work with clients who are very involved—and your prospective client wants to be involved—talk about that. To explain all this, you can show project and meeting schedules, timelines, budgets, and even invoices. These documents demonstrate how you are an advocate for your clients, managing their money and their time, and they show how you will include them in the process through meetings and walk-throughs. It's a huge part of communicating value. They're entrusting you, potentially, with millions of dollars, so you want to be clear about how you'll take care of that money and how you'll take care of them.

Explaining how you staff specific projects and even how you staff your entire office is a huge part of this "how." It helps clients understand what they're paying for—the head count, the skill level, the complete suites of services offered by your various employees. To do this, you can provide examples of staffing lists for projects of similar scale, again offering examples from different

> "Make your billing transparent so that clients understand what they are paying for."
> **NEWELL TURNER**

tiers of pricing, and you can bring key team members to meetings. In fact, I always suggest bringing one member of your staff to an initial client meeting. This makes it clear that you're leading a team that you trust, and it lets clients know from the very start that their project will be supported by other people in your office. (Always be sure to introduce any additional people from your office and explain why they're at the meeting.)

Giving a sense of your overall office structure, meanwhile, goes even further to define the services a client will receive from your staff, and it also explains your firm's overhead. This doesn't have to be a PowerPoint presentation of your firm's org chart. It can be much more subtle. When you show what a typical bill looks like, for example, you can mention your bookkeeper and talk about how he or she will be there to help clients with any questions they have about billing.

GETTING TO THE PROPOSAL

I had a client years ago who once sat me down and said, "We have a problem. We don't know what it is, but we're not winning commissions the way we usually do." I asked him to tell me about his firm's process for getting work, and he explained that he would usually meet prospective clients at the project site and walk the site with them while hearing about the commission. He'd give ideas and let the client know what he thought about the project's potential while they walked around, and then he'd send the client a proposal a few days later.

And I said, "Wow. You send them a proposal after just that initial site meeting?" He nodded. "They haven't even seen your work at this point, and you haven't met with them at your office?" He nodded again.

So I explained that his process was broken. While he'd initiated a process of inquiry to help him understand the project and the client, he hadn't done anything in the way of advocacy. And he had not merely failed to start with his "why"—he had skipped it entirely. He wasn't educating the clients about himself, his passion, and his work, nor relating his past experience to their project. And he certainly wasn't explaining where his fees came from. He was failing to define and communicate his value for these potential clients; that's why they weren't signing contracts with him. And who could blame them? They were receiving contracts and pricing sheets and terms in a vacuum.

"I think you're sending your proposals too soon," I said. "This is a step-by-step process, and you don't want to get to the agreement too soon, but instead build the relationship as much as you can before the contracts stage." The steps I recommended to him then, and to all my clients now, are:

- **Meet the clients at the project site.** This is the **inquiry** stage, when you come to understand all you can about the commission, the clients, and the clients' interest in you, getting as much out of them as you can and asking those key questions mentioned on page 58. Discover the clients' "why."

- **Bring the clients to your office and take them on a tour of your work.** This is advocacy, the point at which you use the three value-establishing strategies discussed earlier to illustrate what clients' money gets them—your "why," your "what," and your "how." Show them your projects; let them understand your processes; introduce them to your team. Throughout this, you'll still be talking about their project, too, of course, learning more about them and their commission as you go. End your time together by saying something like, "Now that we have a great understanding of your project and you understand why we do what we do and how we do it, we'll take a few days to assemble a proposal, which we can then review together."

"To make money, you have to grow—you have to learn how to show other people what you want and let them do it." **GIL SCHAFER**

- **Invite the clients back to review the proposal.** I prefer to have clients and designers review a proposal in person so that the designers can help the clients completely understand it and can immediately answer any questions. Having this interaction together helps both designers and clients figure out whether they do in fact want to work together. Depending on the clients, you may want—or need—to send the proposal in advance of your meeting.

If you shorten this process in any way—and certainly if you skip the "why"—you're much more likely to lose a potential client.

Picking the Right Negotiator

WHO NEGOTIATES

A lot of my clients don't like to negotiate their own fees and terms with clients. They feel that they're the big-picture thinkers, the artists, the creative talents, and that when they have to handle the nitty-gritty of negotiations and contracts, it can muddy the relationship between them and their clients and pull them away from the design work they prefer—and need—to be doing.

But keep in mind, as the principal of your own firm and the person whose name is more than likely on the door, ultimate responsibility for running your practice, and running it correctly, lies with you, even if you don't handle the day-to-day negotiations.

It's worth noting that, in my experience, clients respect you more when they see that you actually run your business, even its financial and logistical sides. All that being said, you can be entirely successful whether you negotiate for yourself or have someone else do it.

I once had a client who always did her own negotiating and whose strategy I particularly admired. She'd take the initial meetings with a client, and when it came down to the contract, she'd say something like, "Let's get through this tough stuff first. We'll get all the expectations and terms done and dealt with, put it behind us, and then we can get to the fun part of just designing your home and really enjoying it." She was able to be her own negotiator because she could divide the negotiating process from the design process; she was able to separate them temporally—first the deal, then the design—but also, it seemed, psychologically, for both herself and her clients. She compartmentalized them so that one wouldn't interfere with the other.

Developing a strategy like this—whether you negotiate for yourself or not—ensures everything is squared away before you and your client start working together. As I noted earlier in this chapter, you never want any surprises or changes to the rules along the way. It's best to walk the client through the entire contracting process and get it all ironed out before you get to the fun part, as my client put it. Only then do you move forward.

Many people, of course, just don't want to be their own negotiator—or they find they can't be, because they simply don't have the talent or skill for it. If that's the case for you, then you need to find the best senior person on your staff to do the negotiating for you. Then, when a client asks you about fees, you can immediately explain that you don't talk about them, but your colleague does. This could be your CFO, controller, or business manager, though I wouldn't suggest you use your bookkeeper. You can even rely on an outside consultant or agent. (I handle client negotiations for many of my own designer clients, for example.)

Having someone else—whoever it is—do your negotiating provides plenty of benefits. It allows for a more concrete segregation between the design process and the negotiating process. This can not only prevent your creative relationship with clients from getting sullied by talk of money, it can also give clients the opportunity to open up about any concerns they may have that they don't want to share with you, the designer. You're giving them access to another person who can be an agent for you and allay concerns—especially ones that might have to do with you.

GOOD COP / BAD COP

Having a separate negotiator also lets you play the classic game of good cop/bad cop. It's a dance I engage in with my clients and *their* clients all the time.

As soon as the subject of money comes up between one of my clients and a prospective client of hers—and it tends to come up early and often, because she's known for doing high-end, high-profile work for rock stars—she says, "I never talk about my fees! Talk to Keith." And then I'm the one who says, "Let me tell you about the terms of working with her..."

This separation allows her to play good cop to my bad cop. Clients may mention to her that I've come in at a price they consider quite high, and she can then respond sympathetically with, "Oh, you know, he's always so tough. Let me see what we can do," and maybe even suggest that she could lower her fees or make her terms easier. But she'll then call me, tell me what she's proposed, and say, "But there's no way I actually want you to agree to that." And when the client comes back to me, I say we can't work with those fees or terms.

Good cop/bad cop lets you give the impression of bending, or maybe even *actually* bend, if you really want to, but also provides you with an excuse when you don't want to give in. You can say it's all the bad cop's fault and stay above the fray, at least as far as the client knows.

Learning the Art of Saying No

Saying no to a project is one of the hardest things for designers. We fear that the next project will never come along or we think that a project we have a bad gut feeling about could turn out to be something major. As a result, we take projects that may not be right for us; indeed, they may be completely wrong.

Knowing *when* to say no comes down to introspection, to figuring out the criteria that make you say yes to a project and then saying no when a prospective commission doesn't meet enough of those criteria. The specifics of developing and using these criteria will be the subject of sections in Chapter Three, "The Marketer," and Chapter Six, "The Things Only You Can Do." A lot of it, as you might expect, comes down to the alignment of your "why" with the clients'.

Here, however, I want to talk instead about *how* to say no. The goal of your "no" should be to put clients at ease, to make them still feel embraced, not outright rejected. You want to leave clients with positive feelings; you never know when a better opportunity may come up to work with them again, and you never know whom they might refer to you in the interim—or *not* refer to you if you leave them with a bad taste in their mouth.

First off, you want to give clients a good reason, ideally one that's as honest as possible. One gentle excuse is to tell clients it's a question of a project's scale and your firm's current bandwidth. Very often you tell clients you're just too busy to take on their project. (If it really is the case that you're too busy to take on a project, and it is one that you want, always consider moving things around or bringing on more staff; while some clients will wait for you, most will not.) You can also tell clients that the aesthetic of their project—but never their *personal* aesthetic—isn't a match for your work right now. I've gone even further, however, saying that I didn't think I was philosophically aligned with a client. That can seem a bit harsh, but if it's true, the clients may feel the same way themselves.

Whatever reason you provide, the key second step to saying no nicely and softly is to refer these clients to someone else. It helps the clients, who may be at a loss as to where to go next, by placing them in the care of someone you trust. Referring work also builds your reputation within your community of colleagues. It's a simple case of paying it forward: every piece of business you refer to a colleague earns you future referrals.

What You Can Give Away and What You Must Never Give Away

As I said in the introduction to this chapter, negotiating your fee is not an option. Lowering your prices has a much bigger effect on your firm than simply losing you money. It tells clients that you don't value your own skill and talent and that you can be had for whatever price *they* think is acceptable. **If you let people think your fees are negotiable, then they'll think your talent is negotiable.** And that eats away at your integrity and the respect you seek to earn in the industry.

Discounts do everyone a disservice. You can explain to potential clients that if you always charge 15 percent of construction costs—as is typical in the industry (see previous chapter)—and someone comes in and negotiates you down to 12 percent, then you will think about that missing 3 percent every time you work for that client, and maybe even kick yourself for it. Because of human nature, you're likely to either become resentful of that client or skimp on the time and the work you put into that project so that the energy you expend is more proportional to the money you're making. Every client I've ever explained this to has responded with something like, "You're right. Why *would* I put you in that position? And why *would* I want that treatment? That's awful."

You won't win every time, of course. It certainly happens that you refuse to negotiate your fees and a potential client just walks away. But I've seen it happen again and again that you hear back from clients who went with a designer who gave them a lowball estimate, and they tell you they ended up spending exactly what you'd told them it would cost. The result? They'll never go back to that lowballer, but they may come to you for their next project—or refer people to you—because they respect the fact that you were honest with them.

Remember: it's better to let a client walk away than to cut your fees.

And when your fees are appropriate, as they will be if you follow the guidelines in the previous chapter, you may even find that the client comes back to you.

SO WHAT CAN YOU GIVE AWAY?

I know what you're thinking: you want to know what *is* up for negotiation. The fact is, nothing really should be, at least nothing involving fees.

Take, for example, the markup on reimbursable expenses. Clients often push back on this, because they don't see why you should get 15 percent on the money you spend on their behalf, on things like flights, rental cars, or cabs; on overnights in hotels when you make site visits; or even on the printing of plans and renderings. But I explain to clients that the 15 percent barely covers the cost of administering those expenses, which includes the salary of a bookkeeper and the time it takes for your staff to track the billings, send out bills, and follow up. A designer's out-of-pocket expenditures also can affect a firm's tax and insurance burden. Clients need to know this.

If they still want to trim these costs, the answer isn't to reduce your markup but to explain to clients that they can pay for all of these expenses directly. A client can pay in advance for your flights and hotels, for example, or even cover printers' costs. If your firm never has to touch or see these expenses, you don't have to charge the extra 15 percent.

Beyond the markup on reimbursables, here are a few other points that designers often see as negotiable but that really aren't:

- **Site visits** Designers frequently think that they can cut their fees by limiting their visits to a site. This is risky, however, because if you are not checking in on a regular basis, you may lose control over how contractors or fabricators are interpreting your drawings and what they are actually building. You have ultimate responsibility; your name is on the line, so limiting your visits to lower your fees is a false economy. You've got to be on site.

- **Photographic rights** If you give up the right to photograph a project, agreeing to a demand from a client who is particularly private, you'll have no way to share it with other potential clients who might be interested in seeing your completed work. It's up to you to decide if the project is still worth taking on (see Chapter Three, "The Marketer").

- **Ownership of documents**   Your drawings should always be your intellectual property. It may not seem like a big deal, but I can cite plenty of instances in which an architect gave up rights to her drawings and the client took them and built in a place other than where the structure was originally intended. The building then failed, and the architect got sued.

- **Discounts based on economy of scale**   There are times when projects grow so large that you could see savings from your vendors on purchases of materials, but, at least with residential architecture, this doesn't really occur until you reach a minimum of $5 million in construction costs.

CUTTING COSTS

If your proposal is well over the clients' budget, it may be that you're just too expensive for them, but if you've set your fees appropriately, it's just as likely, if not more likely, that the clients' budget doesn't match the scope of the project. If that's the case, the way to trim costs isn't to cut your fees; it's to explain to the clients that they may need to change the scale and scope or the timeline for what they want you to do—a smaller project or one with less luxurious finishes or one that goes slower and takes longer should have a smaller budget. There's an old adage that clients need to pick two out of these three: fast, cheap, and good (or, as I like to say, time, value, and quality). They can have a short timeline and good value, but the quality will be lower; or they can have high quality and good value, but it will take a long time. If they want a short timeline *and* high quality, then they'll need to sacrifice the value proposition. They just can't have all three.

One final note: Although it may seem like a good strategy, I don't recommend coming in with a higher number—asking for 18 percent of construction costs, say— just so you can negotiate down to 15 percent. Coming in so high runs the risk of a client just walking away when every other bid comes in at 15 percent, and it's also disingenuous.

Key Phrases

- When starting with "why": *We build beautiful work because we believe that our designs can _____.* (For example, a firm's "why" might be a belief that the firm's designs can "lift the human spirit"; you'll fill in your own.)

- When clients wonder how involved they need to be: *A house is a product; a home is a process. If you want* your *home, then you need to be involved in the project.*

- When moving into the agreement stage of the process and negotiating: *Let's get through this tough stuff first, finalize the contract, and then we'll be free to get to the fun part: designing your home.*

- When a client asks for a reduction of your fee: *Why would you put me in a position where everyone else is getting one price and you're getting a discount? How is that fair to all my other clients? And you certainly don't want to be treated like a second-class citizen in our office.*

- When a client objects to a markup on materials: *You don't go to Nordstrom and expect to pay the same price for a pair of shoes that the store's wholesale buyers pay, so why would you expect your designer to pass along the volume discount he receives from his vendors?*

- When hiring an employee: *I think you are worth more than you asked for, so I'm going to give you slightly more than you requested in the hope that you will prove me right.*

- When negotiating with vendors or subcontractors: *We want to build a long-term relationship with you, and what we expect in return are your best rates and best services.*

- When saying no to a client: *Let me tell you why we are not right for your project*…Then, if it's that the budget doesn't fit, say so; if it is a mismatch in design aesthetic, say so; if it is a fit but you just have a bad feeling, then say you are too busy! *I don't believe we can deliver the project you are after with the budget you have established, and we would not want to disappoint you; therefore, we will pass on your project*, or *Your project seems to be outside our aesthetic reach, and we think you would be better served by a designer like _____.*

Remember, the term "negotiator" doesn't mean compromise, it doesn't mean used car salesman, and it doesn't mean cutthroat hard-ass; what it means is conviction and a strong belief in your value. You have to believe in yourself and your talents before anyone else will believe in you. Learn how to understand the people you are negotiating with before you begin to promote your talents, and you will be able to navigate yourself into better fees, better projects, and better relationships.

YES BUT

Yes with the word **"but"** after it
negates the idea that
was just presented to you

YES AND

Yes with an **"and"** following it
builds on the idea that
was just presented to you

CHAPTER THREE

The Marketer: Promoting Your Practice

IN THE FIRST TWO CHAPTERS of this book, I talked about various negotiating and finance roles and responsibilities, many of which you can delegate to high-level members of your team and their staff. But when it comes to marketing—the focus of this chapter—you, as your firm's principal, really have to run the show. There will be plenty of tasks that you can delegate, but the primary marketing functions belong to a firm's principals, who will also mentor key individuals to allow them to join in marketing efforts. In larger firms, your ability to delegate will depend on the person you have in place as a marketing coordinator.

Although employing a great marketer is essential, that person will never substitute for *you* as the owner of the company and the face of the business. Clients want to meet you; colleagues need to see you; editors have to hear from you. They all want *your* point of view, and presenting that is a huge part of your role in running your firm.

At the end of the day, you are the one most capable of selling your talent.

What Marketing Is and Why It Matters

Before we go any further, let's take a step back and define marketing and then look at what makes it important to your firm's well-being. **FIG 3.1**

At its most basic level, marketing is getting yourself out there, making yourself known. It's about ensuring that you, your firm, and your projects are top of mind with whoever is going to refer you more work. It encompasses such seemingly disparate elements of your business as your professional networks and client relationships, your magazine placements, your website, your social media accounts, and your participation in events such as show houses—even the look and feel of your office's lobby and the way your staff answers the phone—and much more in between, too. But it all comes down to the same thing:

You never want to be anyone's best-kept secret.

MARKETING PLAN OUTLINE

1 Understanding your core: why you do what you do

2 Articulating your vision and mission statements

3 Setting goals
   a Year 1
   b Year 2
   c Year 5
   d Year 10

4 Understanding your audience

5 Defining the services you offer

6 Laying out a public relations strategy
   a Hiring a PR agent
   b Identifying the most interested employees to engage
   c Creating or redoing website
   d Developing a press strategy

7 Understanding your competition

8 Planning business development strategies

9 Identifying new opportunities/ services/disciplines

10 Budgeting

11 Creating a timeline

12 Assessing staffing needs

13 Identifying champions for each goal

14 Developing criteria for how you will measure your success

3.1 An outline for the components of a marketing plan

Building a business means bringing in more—and more important—projects, but it's much tougher to actually run your business and do the creative work you love if you're constantly having to pound the pavement or pick up the phone in search of new commissions. The "why" of marketing, then, is to minimize that pavement pounding and cold calling. The idea is to keep yourself front and center for all kinds of stakeholders—other designers, real estate agents, contractors, key partners in your business, or anyone else who will bring you work—so that projects start flowing your way.

The question, of course, is how to make this happen.

Here's just one of many ways to begin thinking about marketing: At Granet & Associates, many of our interior design clients would like to work with our architect clients. I constantly remind them that while it's great for an architect to know who you are and to be familiar with your website, that's only the beginning.

If you can send out a monograph, or even just a beautiful portfolio, to sit on someone's desk or in a conference room, then you're ahead of the game. Again and again I've been in a meeting and a client has asked me for an off-the-cuff recommendation, and I've said, "It just so happens that I have three portfolios sitting right here. Let's take a look and see if any of these resonate with you." Nine times out of ten, one of those three gets a call and then gets the job. The key in these situations was that those designers had not only made the effort to send me their portfolio, but also gotten me to understand their thinking and design philosophy. Marketing is about relationships, and these designers did not simply drop off their portfolios, but sat with me to explain how they think, how they collaborate, and how they design. All of this makes it easier for me to recommend a designer for appropriate projects. Getting new work starts from the moment you meet a colleague, even before you send examples of your work and follow up.

SOFT VS. HARD MARKETING

So far, what I've been talking about is something I call **soft marketing**. Soft marketing is building and maintaining long-term relationships: meeting people, giving them something to remember you by, and then reminding them of your talent and success from time to time. It's a largely passive, long-game proposition, based on laying the groundwork for strong, interconnected networks that effortlessly bring you work.

Hard marketing, in contrast, is much more of an eyes-on-the-specific-prize operation. It's often about short-term, active project pursuit—identifying a prospective commission or type of commission and then throwing resources behind getting the client, getting the contract, and getting it done. It involves a much more directed and much more active expenditure of energy.

I generally advise our clients to focus on soft marketing (which this chapter is largely about). I make this recommendation in part because soft marketing requires less immediate effort, but also because it's a more subtle, open way of selling yourself that I've seen produce far greater returns on investment.

But there is a time and place for hard marketing, too. When you hear about a project that ticks all the boxes for your ideal commission (see "Knowing Your Market," on page 85) or when you decide to pivot into a new sort of work, getting business may require more pointed tactics.

For example, an architect client of mine wanted to expand his practice to include more institutional work, so he and his team made it a point to start participating in design competitions to create new buildings for major universities. At first, because they had no experience, they were turned down time after time. But the schemes they created for each submission went into their institutional portfolio, and soon they were able to put together proposals and presentations filled with examples of just the sort of new work they were after. The proposed buildings may never have been constructed, but they represented the high level of ideas and designs the architect could bring to the table. These proposals eventually landed the firm its first project in this space, and it's now very well known for its institutional work.

Another example comes from my days at Gensler, when the firm made its first concerted effort to go after airport work, pursuing major projects that would raise their profile and elevate their design skills. To do so, they didn't just start aggressively promoting the fact that they designed airports, nor did they simply begin responding to requests for proposals for these projects, relating them to the firm's previous other types of work; instead, they smartly recruited a top airport designer, whose hiring brought them not only the experience and expertise they needed but also the connections and relationships required to actually win commissions. After hiring him, they became qualified airport architects almost overnight, and the work they wanted came their way.

Here's a look at the difference between soft and hard marketing, and some of the types of activities that correspond to each:

SOFT MARKETING	HARD MARKETING
Long-term relationship building and maintenance	Short-term, active project pursuit
Identify firms and/or individuals you admire and would like to work with.	Seek commissions that will help your firm grow by working with a particular firm or project type.
Reach out to the people and firms you've identified, introducing yourself and your work, taking them to lunch, and visiting their work or studio.	Answer RFPs (requests for proposals) and RFQs (requests for qualifications), as an opportunity to compete in new marketplaces and for new types of projects.
Send the new contact a physical presentation of your work, likely a book or portfolio.	Pursue involvement with the firms that you most want to work with through direct outreach and cold calling, as well as sending your portfolio.
Join organizations that will introduce you to like-minded colleagues whom you admire.	Attend events organized by companies that are commissioning work.
Use collaboration with other professionals as an opportunity to build relationships with people you want to work with.	Proactively identify the projects that you seek and contact the key individuals responsible for awarding those projects.

HARD MARKETING DOS AND DON'TS

While hard marketing can at times be necessary, it can risk becoming off-putting. There are better and worse approaches, with the worse ones verging on overly aggressive on a corporate level or nagging and annoying on a personal level. The best sort of hard marketing, in contrast, retains elements of the soft sell.

A retail executive once told me that one of the least effective things a salesperson can ask is "Can I help you?" Instead, it's much better to introduce yourself and then say, "If you need anything, let me know." Or even "How can I help you?" This opens the door to many potential responses and makes it harder to just say no. There's a pressure in "Can I help you?"; it implies that customers may get directed to a bunch of products that they don't have any interest in, rather than being able to browse on their own to find what they're actually after. "If you need anything, let me know" allows the customer to have a look around and then reach out with any questions. Customers will ask if they need something or want to know more, but if you assume you can help people and present yourself in a way that reveals that, they may get turned off, thinking you're just doing it for the money and that you don't actually care about the work.

All of which is to say that even hard marketing can be done in a softer manner based on relationship building, even as you target and pursue specific projects—just as it worked with my client's expansion into institutional work and with Gensler's into the airport business.

This is also true at the personal, one-on-one level. I was recently standing with two of my clients at an event, one a nationally famous architect with whom everyone wants to work, the other an interior designer with a strong portfolio, a great following in her local market, and a rising national profile. Apropos of nothing, the interior designer turned to the architect and said, "I just want to work with you. One project, just give me one project." The architect's response to this? "I would love to see your work; call me." But there was something less than genuine in his words; the chance of the architect's actually considering this designer's work for a potential collaboration was slim after her forceful pitch. She needed to instead express her fondness for his work and engender a fondness for her own.

Later, when we were alone, I gave the interior designer some advice about how she might have broached the subject differently with the architect: "He knows you already, so you don't need to talk to him that way." Her approach created the presumption that they were not equals. "What you would have been better off saying," I continued, "is, 'I'd love to get together and show you my portfolio the next time I'm in New York. I think you'd be pleased.' And he would have said, 'Of course.'"

"I just want one project from you" is the equivalent of "Can I help you?" It was a total turnoff because it turned the interior designer into a starving pursuer of work and the architect into her kill.

With hard marketing, you don't want to appear desperate and you don't want to act as though you're beneath the person you're approaching. Instead, be yourself, be considerate, be thoughtful, and let conversations proceed naturally and be open-ended. Identify something you admire about the other person's work that seems aligned with your aesthetic and your projects and mention that, then follow up by sending a friendly personal note with your portfolio or book. This makes it clear you're familiar with the other person's work, and it introduces the idea of your working together. That increases the chance that the person will engage with you and eventually consider a collaboration.

Just think of the different outcome if my interior design client had said, "I've been meaning to tell you since we last saw each other: I love how you handled the interior finishes of that Greek Revival project in your book, to make it seem authentic to its origins but also appropriate to today. I'd love to hear how you developed that design because I'm thinking about something similar for a home I'm working on for some of my favorite clients right now. It's a project I think you'd actually be interested in, as well."

MARKETING AND PUBLIC RELATIONS

No firm's marketing work is complete without public relations, but PR is just one piece of the marketing puzzle. PR is simply the marketing you do to the press, getting yourself out there and in front of editors, writers, and bloggers. (As with all marketing activities, it's vital that you're out there leading this yourself, regardless of whether you have a PR person in-house or are working with an agency—but more on that later.)

The difference between PR and marketing is that PR is the external process of exposing your work to the world at large, while marketing is the internal push to find new work, which is driven by the firm and targeted to more specific audiences of your colleagues, collaborators, and clients, both old and new. The other major defining characteristic of PR is that it usually publicizes completed projects, while more general marketing is about looking for new work.

Who Should Market?

If there's only one thing you take away from this chapter, it should be this:

Every member of your staff—from the mail room to the executive suite—is part of your marketing team.

Yes, you may hire someone or even a few people to take on specific marketing responsibilities, but the best thing you can do to bring in more work is to share the responsibility and empower everyone who works for you to bring in new business. Believe me, it works. And I'm living proof of it.

When I started at Gensler, I was in my early twenties and running the mail room. One day, I was riding the bus from my apartment in Berkeley over to San Francisco because I couldn't afford to live in San Francisco on my mail-room salary. I was making conversation with the woman next to me, and, as often happens, she asked, "So, what do you do?" When I told her I worked for Gensler, she said, "I know Gensler—you sponsor *Masterpiece Theatre* on PBS," which we did at the time. That was all she knew about the firm, however, so she asked me to tell her more. I explained, with all the assurance and authority my twenty-two-year-old self could muster, that we mostly did the interiors of corporate offices and law firms, as well as some architectural projects. As it happened, she was the assistant to the managing partner at a major San Francisco law firm. The office, she told me, had just lost its lease, was looking for new space, and needed to find an architect.

"Do you have a card?" she asked.

And I did.

Because at Gensler, everyone had a business card, even the mail-room jockey.

I handed her my card and told her that while I wasn't the person who'd be responsible for her project, I'd be happy to lead her to the right contact. The law firm eventually hired us, and it ended up being a major commission, one we got because of a bus ride and a business card. (I have similar stories from plane rides, grocery store lines, and cocktail parties.)

That's only part of the story, of course—and not just because Gensler still had to actually win the business. Getting the commission also required me to be proud of where I worked, to be able to talk about the firm knowledgeably, to feel that my contribution to these marketing efforts wouldn't go unnoticed, and to think of marketing as part of my job. And because of the culture at Gensler, all of those requirements were met.

Whenever I would tell this story, people would ask what I got in return for bringing in this bit of business, and I would say, "I got to keep my job." I know it sounds like a joke, but it was true. At Gensler, they all but expected this sort of thing from you; that's why everyone had a card.

But it was also true that everyone got credit: every Friday, Art Gensler, who headed the firm, would have a staff meeting during which he would announce who'd brought in projects. I still remember the afternoon he acknowledged me for bringing in that law firm project, and people said, "Isn't that the guy in the mail room?" His recognition made me feel proud, but his singling me out also made everyone else pay attention to me and think about what *they* might be doing to bring in work, if even the mail-room guy could.

So, do I really think I didn't get anything for landing the law firm other than keeping my job? Of course not. I probably got promoted a lot faster than others. I probably got bigger bonus checks than others. Maybe I got a bigger raise. But there was the understanding on Art's part that everyone would

> "If you don't have people who are united in the way you do business, design projects, market your firm, and interact with clients, you can't grow." OSCAR SHAMAMIAN

be working to bring in business, and everyone on staff understood that they'd be rewarded for it in one way or another. And I've been practicing and preaching a similar strategy to my clients ever since.

FIVE WAYS TO MAKE EVERYONE ON YOUR TEAM A MARKETER

1. Instill pride.

Part of making people proud to work for you is getting the sort of high-profile commissions that earn bragging rights. But just as important is creating a rich and vital, fair and open office culture, in which everyone has a voice and creative contributions are valued. (See more on office culture in the next chapter.)

2. Empower engagement.

Give everyone business cards and encourage them to talk about the firm and what they're working on with anyone who seems interested—or who should be interested. Make sure your entire staff knows about the various projects the firm is currently handling, so they can talk knowledgeably about not just their own work but that of their colleagues, too.

3. Encourage networking.

Give your team the time—and your blessing—to attend conferences, meetings, and events, allowing them to stay in touch with colleagues and former classmates. Suggest new networks they might tap into and professional organizations they might join to expand their reach, and your firm's.

4. Give credit.

Just as Art Gensler did in those weekly meetings, you should publicly thank the people who are responsible for bringing in new projects. This makes it clear that everyone who works for you has a stake in ensuring the firm's growth and financial security. It's equally necessary to acknowledge everyone working on current commissions. It can be our habit to give only a lead designer credit, but whenever possible, point to all the people who work on a job.

5. Reward success.

Make it clear that those who help the business expand will be compensated for it: an end-of-year bonus, a piece of the profit sharing, a better raise, an earlier promotion, or maybe even all of the above. Knowing there's a reward for taking care of the place where they work encourages people to do so.

SPECIFIC MARKETING ROLES

With you leading the effort and everyone on your team empowered to bring in business, your small-to-midsize firm won't need much in the way of employees who work exclusively on marketing and PR.

Should you find that you'd like someone to do the administrative tasks related to new business, you may want to hire a **marketing coordinator** or two. That person or people can support your efforts by following up on requests for proposals and qualifications (RFPs and RFQs); putting together tailored marketing packages to send to architects, interior designers, real estate agents, and contractors; and maintaining and updating your website, reporting useful analytics regarding traffic, click-through, and users' time spent on the site. Your marketing coordinators can respond to initial press inquiries and requests, with you ultimately being the one to follow up with editors and writers. They will even handle your social media accounts, if they can be trained to post in your voice and with your point of view.

It's your responsibility to do proactive media outreach, especially with the important editors at the most established and influential magazines (see "The Media Equation" later in this chapter). They have to know who you are; that's how you get published.

As for bringing in outside PR, even my most successful designer clients usually don't work with an agency until they have a product line or some other specific thing that they really want to promote. If you do hire a PR agency to promote you to magazine editors, most editors will want to talk to you, and only you, as the designer. So even if you have an agency, that doesn't get you off the hook when it comes to getting to know editors, cultivating relationships, and making sure they see the best of your latest projects.

Knowing Your Market

Two of the most important, but often overlooked, strategies for attracting new business opportunities are to define your target market and then focus your efforts on clients who are in that market. This requires up-front time, effort, and introspection, but it's well worth it.

In our industry, too many people think that their next project is *never* going to come along, and so they take on *anything* that comes along. As a result, they wind up working on the projects they think that they *have* to accept and not the ones that they *want* to—and *should*—take on.

One of the first things I ask my clients to do is to identify the top ten things that make a project attractive. These might be anything from a client's being nice and well educated to a project's having good funding to its allowing the firm to break into a new type of work.

Let's look at the criteria for one particular architectural firm:

- Nice people (no explanation needed).

- The project will move the company forward.

- The project will allow us to do our highest-quality work.

- The client is educated and respectful: he or she is engaged and passionate about the project but also understands that we are the experts and will not interfere in the process.

- The client should have a vision or at least a direction that we can help articulate.

- The budget is appropriate for the scope of the project.

- The opportunity will exist for us to pull together the right team (interior designer, contractor, landscape architects, et cetera).

- The project has meaning in other ways beyond just another job.

These criteria help you isolate what you want from new work—and what you don't want. And that, in turn, allows you to know when to say yes to the right projects, and, even more important, when to say no to business that isn't the best for you. **FIG 3.2**

Once you have this list, you can look at any potential project through the lens of these criteria. If it ticks eight or more boxes out of ten criteria, it's a definite yes; four or fewer, a definite no; if it manages to hit five, six, or seven of them, it could go either way and you'll have to assess which criteria are most important. Maybe the six a project meets are the ones that seem most central to you at the moment; if so, go for it.

Once you start to review new business opportunities with these criteria in mind, you'll find it gets easier to bring in projects you really want to work on. First off, you'll be able to more effectively target your marketing. Second, with every completed commission that ticks eight or more boxes, you'll even more effortlessly attract clients who are aligned with your vision. You'll be making yur name with a specific sort of project and a specific sort of client—the kind you want to have—and like-minded folks will take notice.

> "The number one mistake people make is failing to figure out what kind of clientele they want to attract before spending money on marketing." MEG TOUBORG

THE IDEAL CLIENT

CRITERION	Stone	Tope	Vaszauskas	Olsen	Thorne-Walsh
Client is educated and understands the process	✓	✓	✓	✓	
Client is respectful	✓	✓			
Client is passionate/energetic about the project	✓		✓	✓	✓
Budget is appropriate for the scope of the project	✓	✓	✓	✓	✓
There is potential for work we would be proud of	✓	✓	✓	✓	✓
Project will hold our interest	✓	✓	✓	✓	✓
Client has a personal vision		✓	✓	✓	✓
Project will move the firm forward					

3.2   Sample criteria for the ideal client

MAKE NEW FRIENDS, BUT KEEP THE OLD

Always remember that not all new business comes from new clients. Far from it, in fact.

A good rule of thumb, used in the industry for years, is that 85 percent of your work should be repeat business.

That doesn't mean it's all the same clients coming back to you again and again for additional projects. That happens, of course—I call these people "serial builders"— but more often, it's friends of previous clients or maybe referrals from colleagues you've collaborated with before. For our purposes, "repeat business" is anything for which you don't have to expend a lot of energy, or maybe even any energy at all.

Instead, it's all about what you've put into play—all those soft marketing efforts, all your good work on past projects.

With this 85 percent, clients don't need to be sold on who you are; they already know you and your work, and they're ready, or close to ready, to sign on the dotted line.

When it comes to winning that other 15 percent, however—those entirely new clients—you have to establish your credibility. That takes significantly more time, more work, and more energy, which is why you want to limit it to only a small fraction of your business. If you have to cold-call and then pedigree yourself from scratch for more than 15 percent of your clients, you won't have time to do your actual design work for existing clients. In either case, the work doesn't just come in because you are qualified; it comes because there is a connection between you and your client. If you are the runner-up for a commission with a new client, it generally has much less to do with your qualifications than with the fit between you and the potential client and how you interacted during the vetting process.

The differences between a repeat client and a new client ▶

Servicing your existing clients matters, because they're leading to 85 percent of your work. That's why **client maintenance**, **customer service**, and **communication** are of the utmost importance.

Remember: just because you have a client doesn't necessarily mean you're going to keep that client. Rainmaking—the art of bringing in work—is as much about taking care of existing clients as it is about finding new ones.

Design is a relationship business, and that means tending to relationships by keeping up your services; focusing on clients' needs; and staying in communication before, during, and after projects are finished.

Coming back to that idea of serial builders—these are the patron clients who come to you for their main house, then a summer house, followed by their third and fourth

"The best clients are the ones who are truly engaged. They stay out of your way, but they are truly engaged." NEWELL TURNER

TASK	REPEAT CLIENT	NEW CLIENT
Meeting the client	The client already knows you and your work. The sell can be soft, and the client comes to you with a sense that you are the right designer for the project.	You need to sell yourself and prove yourself. The client doesn't know who you are or much about your work. The sell is hard, and you have to assume the client has several other designers in mind, including those who may be more qualified.
Presenting your work	The client is very familiar with your work or has even worked with you in the past. The presentation should show your latest work and how your firm has evolved. It could even be related to previous work you did for the client.	You need to put your best foot forward to show both relevant work and your most impressive work to get the potential client to believe in your skills. You may also want to talk about publications and awards.
Building a relationship	The relationship has already been built.	You need to show the client what it would be like to work with you and your firm, giving an authentic, true presentation of process and personalities.
Establishing trust	Trust has already been established.	Listen carefully before you start selling yourself, asking insightful, open-ended questions to understand the client generally and the project specifically. Make sure you know what the client is looking for before you sell yourself, so you can tailor your response to the client's needs.
Follow-up	Send a thank-you note with a message about how nice it is to work with repeat clients, and your specific excitement about and interest in the forthcoming project.	Send a note thanking the client for his or her time and offer to be available for any follow-up questions. To show your engagement, pick something particular that the client mentioned during the meeting and elaborate on that idea.

homes, their boat, and their jet. My clients have been working with some of these patrons for decades, and these are the contracts that keep them in business. But even these aren't sure things or forever propositions; even these long relationships require constant cultivation.

I know an architect who had worked with a reasonably well-off pair of patron clients for decades, building their homes as they could afford them. One day, they came into a tremendous amount of money and dropped him for a famous name. Now, maybe they just wanted bragging rights, but they told their former architect—who had his own rising profile—that they felt he just kept doing the same thing for them, and they wanted to work with someone who could take things a step further.

To the architect, this news came out of nowhere. But if a relationship sours, there are usually signs, and there's always a reason or a series of reasons. Maybe both the client and architect start taking the relationship for granted. No matter how familiar you become, it is still a relationship and one that needs to be nurtured constantly. You must stay in tune with the other party to keep it moving successfully. In the example above, it was probably a result of the architect's inability to see some warning signs, failing to nurture the relationship, and taking it for granted. The architect could have pushed the envelope a bit with his clients by offering more variety in his designs for them, and he could have made it more of a regular practice to solicit feedback from them at the end of a given project or before starting a new one. He could have made sure they were more aware of his growth and his other commissions. The clients could have expressed their aesthetic evolution and their desire to have the architect try something different, valuing him enough to give him the chance to show them something new.

Like any relationship, the one between a designer and a client requires work; it needs easy, open discourse and it has to be maintained to thrive and grow.

CULTIVATING YOUR COMMUNITY

Beyond clients old and new, the other key audience you'll want to target is your collaborators, both current and potential. The importance of your relationships with your colleagues can't be overstated. If you can keep yourself in the minds of your fellow professionals across the industry, you will procure projects from them, and they, in turn, will procure projects from you.

As discussed earlier in this chapter, a big part of getting yourself to be top of mind, and then staying there, is having great materials that are beautifully executed and effortlessly accessible. Even in our ever-more-digital age, these materials should exist as physical objects. As good as a website might be, it still forces someone to remember who you are in order to get to it. A book or portfolio sitting on a table or a shelf in a conference room or on someone's desk—especially during client meetings—is a constant reminder that you are out there.

But those physical materials are just the tip of the iceberg. There are much more organized forms of networking: joining professional organizations, attending conferences and other events, participating in charity show houses, and sitting on boards and panels.

Whatever form it takes, however, cultivating a community of your colleagues and building relationships with them ultimately comes down to generosity.

When I cofounded the Leaders of Design Council four years ago and the Design Leadership Network seven years before that, our goal was to create a resource for all aspects of running a creative business and a forum for sharing information and best practices. Many people thought, however, that the organizations and the conferences we planned wouldn't work. "You have all these highly competitive people in the industry who all compete for the same work," I heard. "They're going to get together, get along, and share information? Come on!"

But I believed that on a very deep level, people want to—no, *need* to—talk to each other about how to run their businesses. And you know what? Once we began mounting our conferences, people checked their egos at the door. They really and truly share during these events, and with a generosity of spirit that surprises even me.

Now the Leaders of Design Council has become an organization not only for sharing *information* but also for building community and, as a result, for sharing *work*. For its members and also the broader industry, the council has become a way to communicate the value of good design throughout our profession.

After getting to know each other at our conferences, like-minded people of similar disciplines will call each other and say, "Look, I'm really swamped. I've got a project I just have to hand off. Are you interested?" Or an architect will email an interior designer she liked at our Berlin meeting and say, "I've been looking at more of your work, and I think we'd be great together on this commission I've just gotten." Or a designer looking for a lighting vendor and considering five possibilities will give the contract to the one she met at a conference because there's a familiarity and a loyalty there.

I could tell countless stories of work finding its way to designers because of relationships formed through this community and other similar organizations. (In my first book, *The Business of Design,* I recommend some of the best organizations.)

The professional community you build strengthens your practice. It gives you access to peers around the country and around the world. It allows you to share your work with like-minded colleagues. And, ultimately, it leads to new resources and work for your firm.

BEYOND YOUR COMMUNITY

Networking encompasses other groups, both those you've previously established—classmates, teammates, friends, family—and ones you seek out for personal or professional reasons.

One of the most successful things Gensler did when I was there was to place people who had interest in other industries on nonprofit boards in those fields. The firm put me on the board of the One Act Theatre in San Francisco. I had a passion for theater, but I had absolutely no talent and no real experience on the stage or even in theater administration, so at first I wasn't sure what I could bring to the board. It quickly became clear, however, that the theater could very much use my budgeting and financial-oversight skills, and my fellow board members were happy to have me around.

A year into my tenure there, the director of the theater announced that we'd just lost our lease and needed to move. "Does anyone know an architect?" he asked.

Well, there I was, and, soon enough, Gensler was designing a new home for the One Act Theatre in San Francisco.

When you put people on boards, you expose members of your team to another field *and* you expose the organization to what you do, all while helping a deserving nonprofit. You're putting your firm and your work in front of a group of people whom you might not otherwise come across. The potential for new work lies not just with the nonprofit but with the board members themselves, as well as their friends, family, and colleagues.

Join these boards because they run organizations that you think do good work, but stick around because—you never know. The next thing you hear could be "I have a house…"; "My mother has an apartment…"; or "My boss wants to build a new place in the country…"

The Media Equation

Not so long ago, gaining media exposure meant little more than getting yourself and your projects featured in magazines and newspapers, or maybe buying advertising space in your local market. Today, of course, the media landscape has completely changed, having grown more and more complex at an increasingly rapid pace and continuing to do so. And that can be both good news and bad.

More outlets means there's more room for your work to be seen by more people: in magazines, both print and online, and on blogs, websites, social media, and beyond. With many of these platforms—especially your own website and your social media accounts—*you're* in control of the messaging, even though you may have little say in who receives it.

These days, it's easier than ever to present yourself as you want to be presented, and you can do so quickly, directly, and broadly. The flip side to all the rewards of this exposure, however, is the risk of overexposure. How do you become a favorite of *Architectural Digest* or a social media darling or a household name without making people say, "Oh, her again"?

The answer lies in your being curatorial, careful, and considerate in your approach, always keeping in mind the clients, colleagues, and additional communities you're reaching.

Let's take a look at the current media landscape, starting with the platforms you have the least control over, working our way to those that give you the most agency.

EDITORIAL OUTLETS, BOTH PRINT AND ONLINE

It's the print magazine world that has probably changed the least in recent years, even if publications now have their own websites and social media accounts—a very good thing for you, since some of them post upwards of twenty new stories a day, and they need content.

In the United States, *Architectural Digest* and *Elle Decor* remain the Holy Grails of nationally distributed interiors magazines, as do *House Beautiful, Veranda, Interior Design, Luxe,* and *Cottages & Gardens,* read by both people in the design industry and the general public. While these shelter magazines are most likely the best places to turn readers into clients, don't forget that top fashion, luxury, and lifestyle magazines—from *Vogue* to *WSJ, Town & Country* to *T, Robb Report* to *Departures*—also feature design and have the potential to reach different audiences.

If you're not initially successful in reaching the Holy Grail interior design magazines, the next-best placements are in local publications. Many of these are trusted sources for clients, with audiences that are both targeted and influential in your marketplace.

When you're breaking into any of these, it's all about getting noticed by, and developing relationships with, the magazines' top editors. They remain the ultimate gatekeepers for all the projects featured. That's why it's so important that you handle most of the outreach and interaction yourself—they want and need to know you personally. Maybe at first you'll be quoted about a trend or there will be a small story in a "front-of-book" section of the magazine, and then, eventually, a feature. In terms of getting prominent placement in the Holy Grails, it's often best to work your way up, from a local to a regional to a smaller national publication and, ultimately, to *Architectural Digest* and *Elle Decor*.

That's how one of my clients, the Atlanta-based Suzanne Kasler, did it. She found she had a great champion in *Southern Accents,* which published several of her projects. This led to *Elle Decor* inviting her to create a space in its annual "Design on a Dime" showcase in New York City. From there, the magazine went on to feature her work in its pages. Soon she could lay claim to several national magazine stories, and that led to her meeting Paige Rense, the longtime editor in chief of *Architectural Digest,* who brought her into the fold. Subsequently, Margaret Russell, the magazine's current editor in chief and the former editor of *Elle Decor,* named her to the AD100, *Architectural Digest*'s yearly list of design thought leaders.

(Designers often ask me whether they should do show houses—whether they lead to enough work to make them worth the time, effort, and expense. The answer, I'm afraid, is usually "Not really." A show house can get you recognized by people in the industry, but it rarely directly brings in clients. When a show house is affiliated with a magazine, however, it can have more power—as it did for Kasler. Not only is it good for immediate PR; if you're asked to participate in a show house by a magazine that hasn't featured one of your projects, you can get your foot in the door by playing along.)

Projects find their way into the long-form feature section of a magazine (known as the "well") in many different ways. Sometimes a photographer with a connection brings the project to the attention of an editor; other times a famous client catches the interest of a publication. On occasion a unique element of the work will help the project fit into a magazine's editorial schedule. Often the feature comes about when a magazine does an issue devoted to designers' homes; many of my clients have gotten published because their own houses were so compelling.

The following is a list of key steps toward getting published and some pitfalls to avoid along the way:

- **Have great images.** Often people think that scouting shots are acceptable, but if they are not professional and don't convey the beauty of your work, the project may get rejected without merit. Make sure you present the project in the most positive light.

- **Keep exclusivity in mind at all times.** Images of a project appearing in another magazine can immediately derail its chances with one of the Holy Grails. If you intend to publish a project, keep all images private until you're ready to submit them for consideration. This applies to blogs and even your own website or the client's. Align with your clients; if they understand your publishing goals from the beginning, they can help to protect the project until it is published, keeping finished photography and even process images out of the public eye.

- **Use the best contacts and connections to expose your work.** You can get your project to the right magazine with the help of personal relationships with editors, writers, or photographers who work for the magazine. You may not always know the editors, but you need to be able to show your work in person; explaining the project yourself goes a long way.

- **Study design magazines to understand what makes a project right for each and submit to only one magazine at a time.** If you think you have an *Elle Decor* project, then submit it only to *Elle Decor;* if it is a *House Beautiful* project, then submit it only to *House Beautiful.* Submitting a project anywhere and everywhere may frustrate editors and make them feel that you don't understand their magazine. Tailoring your pitch to a specific magazine shows you're paying attention and that you respect the publication and its editors.

  Further, if you submit to multiple magazines and two of them select you, your relationship with the magazine you don't ultimately give the project to may end. The last thing you want to do is create a reputation for shopping a story around to anyone who will publish your work. Loyalty matters.

- **List and rank the publications most suitable for the project, and submit the project in that order.** This list will help you understand where the project should be placed. Where it points may surprise you; it could help you realize that placement in a local publication will be more effective than in a national one.

- **Follow up with a note** after meeting with an editor or after someone submits a project on your behalf, to show your appreciation for the referral.

One of the greatest frustrations for designers is not being able to get their work published without the consent of clients. This is something you should establish from the very beginning of your relationship; you can even negotiate this in your contract. Often celebrities will stipulate that they don't want their home published because they don't want their privacy compromised, but other very private clients simply may not want their project to be exposed. This obviously means your work won't be seen by as many people, but keep in mind that these high-profile clients can and will recommend you for work with their equally high-profile friends. As alternatives, you could ask whether they'd agree to publishing it as long as their names aren't attached or whether they'd mind including the house in a book rather than in a magazine.

But Does It Work?

Being published doesn't always directly translate into more work, so there are those who question its effectiveness. I've had clients who feel they have never had a commission that they can trace back to a published project, and then I've had others who have had a stranger walk into their offices clutching a year-old magazine that featured one of their projects.

Either way, having your projects out there, especially in one of the top-tier national or even local outlets is, at the very least, a surefire way to make certain that people will see your work and get to know your name. It also goes a long way toward establishing credibility with those 15 percent of clients who provide brand-new business, while giving existing clients something to crow about—"Did you see my designer featured in *House Beautiful*?" And within the industry, among your colleagues, it is a major calling card.

THE SOCIAL MEDIA CHALLENGE—AND IT *IS* A CHALLENGE

Of all the ways in which the media landscape has recently changed, it's social media—especially Pinterest, Facebook, Houzz, Twitter, and, more than any other platform, Instagram—that represents the greatest disruption, mostly for the better, I think, and only occasionally for the worse. **FIG 3.3**

I say it's for the better because it gives you the opportunity to build a truly new audience from the ground up, while directly interacting with current clients and colleagues in a very visual, interactive, and dynamic way.

3.3 a DesignersAxis on Instagram

3.3 b DesignersAxis on Twitter

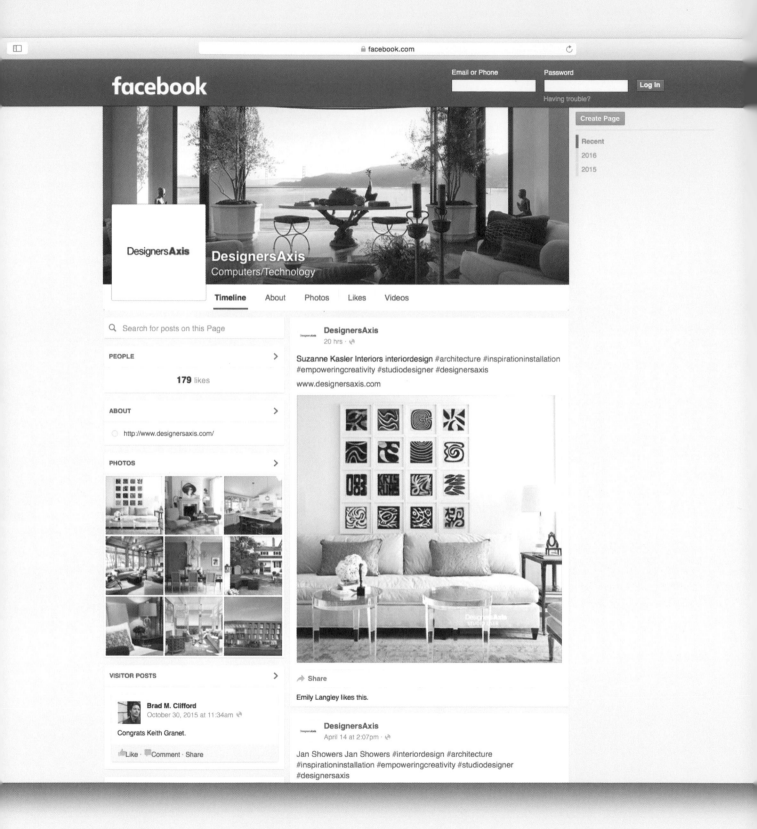

It also grants you a large measure of control over your communication. *You* determine what you post, and, to some extent—depending on the site—you determine who sees it. But even with the tightest of privacy controls, you should assume that anything you post can, and will, be seen by any- and everyone, any- and everywhere; it's going to be repinned and reposted and pushed and pulled every which way. That's the potential danger of social media, even as it's also one of its greatest potential benefits. And that's why strategic, consistent curation is so important. It's all about how you use the medium to get out your message.

You need every post you make on social media to represent you as you'd like to be seen so that no matter where it ends up and no matter who sees it, it sends a positive message about you and your brand.

At Granet & Associates, we have a high-end client, Studio William Hefner, who's had one of the most popular kitchens on Houzz. The firm has been awarded more than one $5 million project on the strength of this one picture. They tend to generally shy away from social media, but they also understand the importance of being out there. They do incredible work, and they selected an impeccable picture to show that off; they'd already gotten good feedback on the photo in the analog world before they put it out there in the digital world, and the internet rewarded them for it.

One of my most published clients is the designer Celerie Kemble. That's not just because she is photogenic, nor simply because her work is beautiful. It's also because she is very smart about what she puts out in the digital world. She has built a strong social media presence, leveraging some of her influential friends, and she has posted as many images and stories of her life and lifestyle as she has of her work. Her multifaceted approach to social media has fed the fantasies of her followers, and it has often led to her phone ringing with new commissions.

The potential downside of such a social media strategy is the overexposure of your life at the expense of your work. If, in the course of a month, you have posted every meal that you have eaten at a fancy restaurant and every private plane that you have flown on and loads of images of designs other than your own, you may find that you very quickly turn your audience off, losing followers and failing to attract new ones.

The key to sharing any message is authenticity. Even if you have a wonderful eye for good work, showing too much of other people's projects is never a productive strategy. It is perfectly fine to pepper your feed with the work of those you admire most, just as long as it is not a constant and there's no misunderstanding that it is something you authored. Always give credit where credit is due.

SIX TOP INSTAGRAM STRATEGIES

1. The camera is king.

Post only perfect pictures. You are serving an audience of highly visual, highly discerning people. Having great imagery can make or break you. This is as much—if not more—about composition, styling, and lighting as it is about filters.

2. Be authentic.

Find your brand's true voice for social media and stick with it. Make sure that it matches your brand outside of the social-media sphere and that it feels consistent with the rest of your story, your work, and your firm's culture. Social media can be an easy disguise to wear. If you're good at it, you can fool a lot of people, but if you lack authenticity, it will be obvious when clients hire you, and you will fail.

3. Context matters.

Showing in situ, fully realized interiors is the way to go. I am now one of the major owners of a software company called DesignersAxis, and one of the original investors in Pinterest sits on our board. She pointed out to me that a big part of Pinterest's success—the reason it works—is that more and more people shop and buy based on vignettes, not on catalog-style silhouetted images. Beautiful images of beautiful rooms—that's what people are looking for. They're thinking, "How do I make my room into that room?" It makes sense that people are inspired by seeing completed rooms, because design is more about the whole than its parts. If you have high-quality imagery of your completed projects (or, in the case of a product line, photos that show your pieces as they might be seen in real life), then people will hold on to that memory and dream about that look or that piece until they can afford it.

4. Consistency is key.

Sticking largely to design—yours and that of people and places you admire—makes for a successful feed. There's a place for the odd travel or food or other lifestyle shot, maybe even a selfie (Instagram loves a selfie), but these can dilute your account and, by extension, your brand. If you have multiple people posting in addition to yourself—a business partner, a marketing coordinator, or others in your office—make sure you're aligned on voice, photo content, and aesthetic. Consistency is a major consideration when it comes to how you write your captions and even your hashtags, as well as the frequency and timing of your posts. Posting on the same day or even at the same time each day or day of the week creates an expectation, and if the content is compelling, you will attract loyal followers and loyal readers.

5. Build your network.

Leverage your existing real-life networks and relationships—with colleagues; with clients; with publications, especially those that have large followings—to build your own.

6. Curate, curate, curate.

Take care with every image as if it might make or break you; consider that each one could very well end up any- and everywhere.

YOUR WEBSITE

The number one place where people go to see your firm's work is your website, so its design and execution matter greatly. **FIG 3.4** What makes for a successful design firm website has evolved over the years—today, video is increasingly used, and sites must now be optimized so that they look just as good on the small screens of mobile devices as they do on a laptop or desktop—but some things remain consistent. Here are a few top-line pointers for a successful site:

- A site needs to be clean, clear, and concise.

- The site's platform must be simple to use and navigate.

- Present information predominantly through images.

- The current trend is to have one long page that users can scroll through easily, discovering more content as they go—like an Instagram feed—rather than to have separate pages that must be clicked through.

- Don't overexpose yourself. If you think you have too many images, you probably do—maybe even double what you need. People who visit your site are looking for your voice, your style, and something special about you. You can offer this through a limited number of beautiful images of a few projects, with brief text.

All of these pointers come back to one thing: people are lazy when it comes to the internet—they are impatient, and, more and more, they will leave your site quickly if they get bored—and if you don't captivate them and make it easy to understand your work, they will leave your site in well under a minute.

I meet a fair number of designers who think it's acceptable to have a social media page instead of having their own website. They tell me to take a look at their work,

3.4 a　Clean and stylish, with large-format images

3.4 b Simple and image-rich

3.4 c   Easy to navigate, with multiple beautiful images

3.4 d   Beautifully presented large-format imagery; easy to navigate

3.4 e   Video is the future for how people absorb content. McAlpine's website does an amazing job of communicating the firm's vision and passion.

and then they give me links to a bunch of boards. I ask where their website is, and they say, "Oh no, that's what I use as a website!"

Having a social media page, whether it be on Pinterest or Instagram or Facebook, is not the same as having a website.

Here's why this is important: I need to see that you've got a real business, and having a real website is a big part of that. Pinterest is an effective way to build an image bank, but don't try to pass it off as more than that. If you want to be treated like a legitimate designer with a legitimate business, you've got to have a website to show off your work, your point of view, your philosophy.

Posting New Projects and Exclusivity

As keen as you may be to post images of a newly completed project as soon as you have finished professional photography, keep in mind that the Holy Grail magazines, and even some a tier down, as well as certain websites, won't consider a project that has been seen, even if only on your own site. And, of course, in this day and age, it's never really *only* on your site. Once it's online, anyone can grab it and post it to Instagram, Pinterest, or Twitter. It may be hard to wait, but doing so is the wisest strategy with a project you hope to publish.

YOUR OWN BLOG OR E-NEWSLETTER

Blogs and e-newsletters can be great ways to disseminate information, but they're also a huge time commitment. If you have time to write a blog, you may not have enough work, which means your time might be better spent on other activities. And many bloggers do not understand basic editorial rules, and therefore their posts are less successful. On the other hand, some people love to write, and they create wonderful blogs. For example, at my client McAlpine, one of the partners, Greg Tankersley, authors the firm's blog. He shows gorgeous images with well-thought-out text, and it very much comes through that he writes not from a sense of obligation but from a passion for design.

Should you decide to devote energy to a blog or e-newsletter, the same social media strategies about authenticity, voice, and consistency also apply here.

In many ways, Instagram may have replaced the blog, but there's one key way that blogs and e-newsletters need to be different from social media: having fresh, interesting, timely, need-to-know content, both visual and written, matters much more. If you want people to read your blog or e-newsletter, it has to be packaged much more thoughtfully, with more editorial shaping. That's because you need people to be interested and devoted enough to click open an email or remember to go to your blog—unlike social media, where the content is fed to them automatically.

To that end, you can show beautiful images of your work and talk about a newsy project of yours, but then you've got to give the reader more, and do so on a regular basis. Maybe it's a great quote; maybe a how-to guide or a best-practices or lessons-learned tool; maybe inspiring images that relate to projects; maybe news and notes and smart observations about current design trends; maybe a Q&A or profile of one of your colleagues or collaborators. The reader needs to keep coming back because you're providing something of interest. It can't all be about selling yourself, because as soon as it becomes too self-serving, you're going to lose your audience's interest.

If people are actually reading your e-newsletter, it's instructive to view the analytics about how your audience uses the info. You can find out what the open rate is and see what images and information people click on. This can help you make decisions about how to design other marketing materials and what images to place front and center on your website, as well as what you might do to improve your social media presence.

The tools we use to communicate our point of view as designers are only getting stronger. With each new innovation we can more effectively connect with our clients. Doing so helps them understand more fully what we do and what we're all about, which engenders a true appreciation of the value of good design. These tools make our relationships with clients stronger, and they open up new ways to market our designs, ourselves, and our firms.

CHAPTER FOUR

Building
the Right Team

I'VE ALWAYS FIRMLY BELIEVED that each one of us is stronger as part of a group than we are as individuals. Thinking and problem-solving collectively can be significantly more powerful and successful than simply relying on your own ideas, skills, and creativity.

In a design practice, that may seem a little counterintuitive. Principals are known for considering themselves the be-all and end-all of their firm—and are often seen that way by those on the outside as well. It's their name on the door, after all. But if you look at the companies run by the most talented and successful aesthetic interpreters out there, you'll always find a strong team supporting them, people with similar points of view and philosophies but different skills.

The fashion world is full of examples of this: a genius creative complemented by someone with a brilliant mind for business, finance, marketing, and more. Consider Yves Saint Laurent and Pierre Bergé, Valentino and Giancarlo Giammetti, or, more recently, Marc Jacobs and Robert Duffy. You can have all the talent in the world, but it can often take a strong business partner to make you successful.

The reason for the success of partnerships like these, and of larger design teams, is that each one of us has a particular skill set, but very few of us (really, probably none of us) have *everything* we need to manage and grow our business all on our own. And so, surrounding yourself with people who complement and augment your skill set in thoughtful and significant ways is of the utmost importance.

Keep in mind: Hiring for different skill sets doesn't just mean bringing in people with diverse specializations and work experiences. It also means looking for people with different points of view and from various backgrounds and supporting them as well as relying on them, according to what they have to offer to you and what they need from you.

> "Be less precious about your own point of view, so you don't close yourself off from somebody else's great idea." GIL SCHAFER

Take, as an example, generational variations. As our life expectancies grow and as people continue working longer, an increasing range of generations find themselves collaborating in the same office. Today most firms have principals who are baby boomers, but coming up quickly are Gen Xers, followed by millennials. This mix can cause occasional tensions, but if you understand each generation's values—both what its members value and the value they can bring to your firm—you'll have a richer and more well-rounded practice.

Baby boomers were taught, and still believe, that if they worked hard—really hard—they would succeed and be rewarded by their employers for their efforts and their accomplishments. Gen Xers, in contrast, believe in leading a more balanced life; they're more entrepreneurial than they are loyal to any one organization. Millennials, meanwhile, are very value oriented and want to collaborate. It is your job to integrate them into your office—to teach them and to help them feel productive, valued, and successful.

A firm's principal will need to understand all of this, as well as each generation's core values, in order to create a collaborative and effective work environment. The baby boomers in your office will have the most experience and may be best at identifying a problem. But it may take an out-of-the-box-thinking Gen Xer or millennial to come up with the most creative, and quite possibly best, solution. Identifying, leveraging, and integrating diverse but complementary skill sets is the key to unlocking the power of your organization, and something to keep in mind when building your team.

This entire book, of course, is about *who* should support you as team members and *why* they're important to making your firm the best it can be. But this chapter, in particular, will teach you *how* to go about creating and supporting this team of diverse thinkers and doers, as well as *when* to expand it.

Hiring the Right People

If I have a mantra when it comes to recruiting and human resources, it's this:
Hire slow. Fire fast.

When you're ready to expand, take the time to figure out exactly what your firm needs and to find the best people to meet those needs. You'll make few hiring mistakes if you do. And, then, if you do find you've made a mistake and someone's not working out, take action to remove that person as quickly as possible. I can't tell you the number of firms I've seen hold on to bad apples for too long, so by the time the principal finally gets rid of the offending employee, that difficult person has poisoned the workplace, maybe even causing good people to leave.

It's well worth it to take your time because it's a huge investment to hire somebody. There's the cost, in dollars and in man-hours, of training someone, and you may have recruiting costs as well. If you don't make wise and thoughtful hiring decisions, you'll end up with a revolving door and your business won't be very profitable.

As I mentioned in Chapter One, "The Financier," there are practices that operate as hire-fire firms, bringing people on and then laying them off as projects come and go. While this may seem expedient and fiscally smart, it compromises the sustainability of your firm and makes it very difficult to establish and maintain any sort of consistent or positive firm culture. It can force you at times to hire anyone you can as quickly as you can, regardless of how well that person fits in with your work and philosophy, and you may also need to get rid of folks you would have liked to keep, just because a project ends. Rather than functioning this way, your firm should operate so that decisions to expand and contract your team can come from a much more holistic assessment of your firm's needs and budgets.

WHEN TO HIRE

Figuring out the right time to expand your practice is a matter of self-knowledge. Deciding when to bring in another designer or a finance type or even an administrative person is all about knowing what is eating up your own time. (For more on self-assessment, see "Your Work Life Is an Onion" in Chapter Six, "The Things *Only* You Can Do.")

Expanding your creative staff is a question of workload: you have too many projects, so you need to bring in additional people to help with the design work, or you're taking on a new sort of project and you want someone with expertise in that arena. But it's also a matter of suitability and efficiency. If you're a designer and you're spending hours and hours each week on management or finance or marketing, then that's taking you away from employing your strongest skill set—your design capabilities—which is how you make money from clients.

The key to smart hiring is identifying the tasks that don't make the most of your current staff's skills or time and then finding people whose general ethos matches your firm's and whose expertise and experience specifically match those tasks.

HOW AND WHERE TO RECRUIT

It's always preferable to hire from within your firm, promoting an existing employee. You'll be stronger and more successful if you can grow your own, so to speak. If you build someone up, he or she will be trained exactly as you want, with the skill set that you need. This isn't always possible, however. You may not have someone who's ready to take on the tasks you need done, either because your current employees simply haven't had enough experience or because you haven't had the time to offer the needed support and mentoring.

If that's the case, then you will need to look beyond your studio. This can be challenging—not because you can't find skilled people, but because skilled people often come with a lot of baggage. They picked up their skills somewhere else, and so they'll have different ways of thinking, different ways of doing things, a different sense of office culture. As I noted previously, you want differences of all kinds in your practice—diversity breeds success—but it can be hard to find the right balance. You want to build a team whose differences complement one another.

There are two main ways to find qualified candidates: you can conduct the search yourself, or you can hire a recruiter.

If you hire a recruiter or an agency, you will pay a fee of anywhere from 15 percent of your eventual hire's annual compensation at the low end up to 33 percent at the high end. There are several serious advantages to using a good head-hunter, however. Recruiters take a huge task off your plate, saving you the time and the energy that you or another member of your team would expend poring over résumés and doing initial interviews to narrow the field of potential candidates. A recruiter should also have more robust resources with which to find candidates. If you're looking to hire a nondesigner—a controller or marketer, for example—then you may not have many personal leads, but a recruiter will. Strong headhunting firms have a ready pool of highly qualified people who are looking to make a move, and they have deep networks to help them find more.

Beyond the cost, there can be a few other challenges to using a recruiter, but if you're careful, you should be able to avoid the potential pitfalls:

- A recruiter should always have your best interests in mind. If the headhunter doesn't really care whether the people he or she finds are good fits with your firm, then you'll just be wasting money. As with any other consultant or vendor, you'll want a recruiter who's thinking about a long-term relationship with you and your firm and about helping you support and strengthen your office, not just about earning a commission.

- The recruiter will need more than just a job description to comprehend who the right candidate will be. Both you and the recruiter need to make sure you have a common understanding of who you are and what your firm is all about. When recruiters get your firm culture, they are much more successful in their placements.

- If a hire doesn't work out and you have just paid thousands of dollars to a headhunter to find this person, you're not going to be very happy. Typically, you'll want the recruiter to guarantee the placement for at least ninety days, but in some cases that trial period can last for up to six months. (After that, though, you'll be on your own; if you haven't figured out after half a year whether a hire is right for your firm, that's on you.)

Here are ten questions to ask a recruiter before you start working together:

- What is your fee structure?

- How long do you guarantee your placements?

- If a new hire leaves before the end of that guarantee period, what happens?

- What if you cannot find the right person for us?

- What is different about your ability to find candidates from what I would do on my own?

- What have been your best sources for finding good people?

- Do you poach from other firms? [If so, you'll need to provide the headhunter with a list of colleagues' firms from which you don't want to poach.]

- How many references do you check, and how do you check them?

- Do you use our firm's name during your search?

- If you don't use our name, how would you handle a situation in which one of our current employees applies for the job?

If you instead choose to handle recruiting and hiring in-house, there are other pros and cons.

The most obvious upside is the immediate cost savings, but keep in mind that every hour you spend recruiting is an hour you could be spending designing and doing other paid work for clients. When you look at it that way, you may be saving much less than you think, if anything at all.

Of course, if you have a human resources manager or an office manager, or even just a good assistant or administrative person who can handle the first round of résumé culling and interviews, you will save a ton of time and money.

Two other advantages to handling this process in-house are that you maintain complete control and you don't have to bring a recruiter up to speed on your firm and your culture, as well as the particulars of this position.

For those who do choose to take this task on themselves, a major hurdle can be finding well-qualified candidates. A few resources are:

- **Your peer groups** I've had clients who have not wanted to spend the money on a recruiter, so instead they have reached out to colleagues. People in your professional network may be downsizing at their own firm or may have an employee who's outgrown a position or looking for a different discipline—or they just might know of someone in the field who's looking but who wasn't on your radar. If you put the word out with your peers that you're looking to hire, usually that shakes enough trees to get a few good candidates thrown your way. An advantage of working this way is that it tends to bring you the sorts of individuals you're looking for because they come from people you trust and who get you already. Like-minded colleagues send you like-minded candidates, which makes this my favorite way to recruit.

- **LinkedIn** Today one of the most powerful business communities is LinkedIn, and many people use it to find employees. (Tomorrow is anybody's guess—maybe we will embed a chip, and when you are looking for a new job you switch it on and all of your skills get broadcasted. Kidding—sort of!)

- **Professional groups** Most industry organizations that support a specific design discipline—the American Institute of Architects, say, or the American Society of Interior Designers—will have an online bank or board where you can post a job listing.

- **Alumni groups** In addition to job postings and candidate banks maintained by your *own* alma mater, there are those of local colleges and design schools. They're all good resources for finding potential candidates.

- **Your website** It's vital that your website have a section about job opportunities, with a "We're Hiring" or "Work with Us" or "Careers" heading and a call to action for candidates to submit their materials digitally. That allows people who specifically head to your site—or even those who end up there while doing more general research—to see that you're looking for staff. You need to keep your listings up to date, however, to avoid soliciting résumés for jobs you don't have open, which can frustrate good candidates. To still bring in great people when there's no currently open position that's right for them, you could consider using phrasing such as: "We are currently hiring for the positions listed here but are always interested in talent. If you think your skills and experience would be a fit with our firm, please submit your résumé and, if appropriate, your portfolio."

The labor pool follows the economy closely; it also follows industry trends. For instance, by 2000 computer-aided drafting and 3-D visualization were very popular. We lost a lot of design students to the entertainment and gaming industries, because the economy for design firms was tanking and the entertainment industry provided lots of opportunities for well-paying jobs, until many of these people got tired of designing make-believe places and wanted to build real buildings or design real spaces and products.

When the economy sinks, so does the job market, and therefore the experience pool shrinks. For example, one of the roles that people are often looking to fill is job captain. This position typically requires five to seven years' experience. From 2007 to 2009, we were deep in a recession so severe that even in the years immediately following nobody was gaining that experience. So by five to seven years later, we were facing a void of people with that level of experience. The ones who do have it have grown and become ingrained in the firms that they're working for, and they're happy to stay at those firms. This creates a vicious cycle in which it becomes difficult to find these resources.

THE INTERVIEW PROCESS

The unfortunate thing about hiring is that, unlike in romantic involvements, you don't really get a chance to date; you just have to get married. And that's why interviewing is so important. It's the closest you get to dating, to getting a sense of how you and a candidate fit together and how hiring that person might work out.

When we show clients choices for design, we limit them to three options, and the same rule exists for introducing potential candidates to the principal. Your outside recruiter or in-house resource needs to do the job of preselecting the top candidates, and they should be limited to three. If there are too many choices, it will be too hard to decide.

Many people ask me where you should interview a potential candidate. It depends: If the candidate is replacing someone whom you will be firing, then you should interview the candidate outside your office. If the position is a new one that you are adding to your firm, then you should interview the candidate in your office and give a tour of your facilities. Remember, the most qualified candidates are interviewing you as much as you are interviewing them.

The first stage of the interview process is to vet the candidates to make certain they have the right skill set. A skilled recruiter or in-house person should eliminate a candidate quickly if the skills and fit don't seem right. Before the candidates meet the principal of your firm their references should have been checked and their salary requirements verified. Your recruiter should make certain that the person the candidate will be working with is part of the process.

The meeting with the principal should be about fit and nothing more. Candidates should bring in any appropriate materials, such as a portfolio and résumé, that explain their strengths. One small secret that I have found successful for younger candidates who may not have a full portfolio of work to share is to ask them to put together a "look book" of the work that inspires them. This enables you to see their eye and whether they are aesthetically aligned with your company.

These are my top ten interview questions:

- What interests you about our firm?

- Tell me about your goals for your career. (This is especially vital for millennials; they want to know you care about their goals.)

- Tell me about your work habits, as well as how you use email and social media, and about your communication skills.

- Do you have any colleagues who have worked here or currently work here?

- Why are you making a change in your employment?

- What do you see yourself doing in five years?

- What skills would you like to improve?

- Have you ever been told anything about your work product that surprised you?

- If there were one thing you could stop doing in your current job, what would it be?

- Who are your mentors?

MAKING THE OFFER

Once you have decided to hire a candidate you will need to make a formal offer in writing; it is important that everyone involved understands what is expected of them. The offer letter should address salary; time off, such as holidays, sick days, and vacation days; health insurance; and any other benefits the firm offers, such as 401(k) or profit sharing and bonus plans. In addition, you need to remind the candidate that he or she is an at-will employee (if that is the law in your state) and that there will be a ninety-day probationary period before he or she is considered full-time and is eligible for your benefits.

Make certain that your candidate is happy with the salary offer. As I recommend in Chapter Two, offer new hires more than what they asked for and tell them that you trust they will prove their worth; they will work even harder to show you that they deserve the higher salary.

NINETY-DAY PROBATIONARY REVIEWS

I strongly believe that new hires should be in a trial period for their first three months of employment, as you get to know each other and see how you fit together. You should make the new employee aware of this from the get-go. At the end of that period, you should sit down with the employee and either confirm their hire or let them go, explaining why. During this ninety-day period employees should earn their full salary, but in many cases benefits may not kick in until after this trial period.

As the ninety-day review period is coming to an end, you will typically check in with the new staff member's supervisor to get an assessment of how things are going, and then you or a senior member of your firm will meet with the employee to ask a series of questions:

- How do you feel you are doing at your job?

- Are you satisfied with the projects that have been assigned to you?

- Do you feel you are being challenged adequately?

- How do you feel about the firm?

- Is there anything we can do differently to help you get acclimated to the office?

If there are any issues you need to bring up or changes that you think the staffer needs to make, this is your time to address them. If a hire is not ready to move out of a probationary period but you still think it is worth keeping that person, you should extend the probationary period another thirty days. If the person is just not working out, you don't need to bother with the questions above—this is the time to terminate.

CONSIDERING CULTURE VS. SKILL WHEN HIRING

When you're building your team, it's essential that you hire first for fit and second for skill.

The reasoning behind this is simple: It's relatively easy to teach new employees the techniques, systems, and practices of your office and to train them in the necessary skill set. It's close to impossible, however, to turn employees who have a completely different philosophy or personality from yours and everyone else's in your studio into the employees you want and need them to be.

So, when you're interviewing candidates, you want to especially be looking for people who seem to have come from a firm with a culture similar to that of your practice or who otherwise seem to have a temperament that's like yours and that of your staff.

Skills are important, too, and the ideal employee will have the skills you need and will also fit into the culture you've established, but starting by interviewing folks who are a cultural fit, even if they may not have all the skills, is still the way to operate—much better than beginning with highly skilled individuals who seem like cultural mismatches.

The chart below helps illustrate this culture versus skills concept. This diagram is an incredibly helpful tool for hiring new staff and evaluating current employees.

FIG 4.1

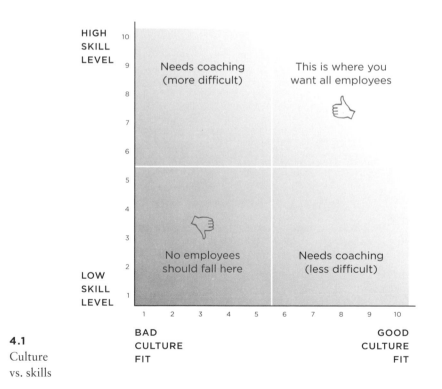

4.1
Culture
vs. skills

On the chart, the *x*-axis represents culture: how well a person fits within your organization in terms of personality, evaluated on a scale of one to ten, with ten being the best. The *y*-axis represents the skill level that you expect that employee to possess—again, on a scale of one to ten, adjusted for relative experience, with ten being the best.

The field created by these two axes is then divided into four quadrants:

- **The bottom-left quadrant** corresponds to the low end of the spectrum, someone with a low skill level who also doesn't fit in with your firm's culture. These people shouldn't be part of your organization at all.

- **The top-right quadrant** has people with a strong skill set who also are great cultural complements to your office. This is where you want all of your employees to be, though it's rare that you'll ever get an entire staff here. Anyone here should be retained for as long as possible and rewarded as much as they can be.

- **The bottom-right quadrant** corresponds to people with a strong cultural fit but low skill level. They need instruction and experience to be brought up to speed. They will need to demonstrate that they can learn and retain the necessary skills, but they are otherwise people you want on your team.

- **The top-left quadrant** corresponds to people with a strong skill level but low cultural compatibility. They need mentoring and coaching, and that can be a heavier lift for you, and for them, than the sort of skills-based training those in the bottom right require. The people here won't fit in at your firm all that well, and it's much harder to overcome the incompatibility caused by that sort of personality mismatch.

I use this tool both when helping firms hire new employees and when assisting them as they evaluate their current staff—and I also use it at my own company. We place potential hires in the correct quadrant based on what we learn from their references, from looking at their portfolios, from their responses to interview questions, and from the overall impression we get by meeting with them. For current employees, we gather information from our day-to-day work together; by talking to an employee's managers, direct reports, and clients; and from the review process, which I'll talk about more later in this chapter. During economic downturns, this tool can be particularly helpful with the difficult task of evaluating whom to retain and whom to let go.

Through working with my clients, I've come to see that a lot about a firm is revealed by where the majority of their staff fall on this chart.

- The firms whose staff mostly land in the upper right, with employees who are good cultural fits and also are highly skilled, are typically the most successful and high performing.

- Firms whose staff mostly fall in the top left tend to be sweatshops. They hire people for their qualifications, not their fit. They produce a lot of projects, and they do so efficiently and effectively, but since the employees are not very synergistic, they also tend to work by themselves, and this lack of collaboration and collegiality results in work that isn't as strong as it could be. Employees who work together well tend to boost one another's creativity, and their designs show this.

- Firms with most of their staff in the bottom right usually have employees who all get along very well, but the offices as a whole often get little accomplished with anything resembling speed, efficiency, or skill. The employees love working there, but they usually aren't extremely successful.

Outsourcing

Sometimes, especially when your practice is still quite small, you can delegate certain roles and responsibilities to outside people or firms. Generally, there are four main areas of a firm's operations that get outsourced:

1. Functions outside of the design sphere

These are the aspects of your firm's business touched on in Chapter One, "The Financier" and Chapter Three, "The Marketer"—a part-time bookkeeper, say, or a public relations agency. Early in your firm's life, or if you yourself are very adept at finances or marketing, you can be successful without bringing these people in-house full-time. There can be real value in hiring consultants who are highly specialized in these roles because they bring extra expertise and a point of view and set of best practices that they've developed from working with many different design firms.

2. Highly technical functions, requiring the latest software skills

There was a big movement about fifteen or twenty years ago, when CAD was really coming into its own as an efficient and increasingly necessary tool, for American firms to send scans of their hand drawings out to companies that specialized in turning those documents into CAD files. Often, these were outfits in Asia; this not only had the advantage of costing less money but also meant that you could send your drawings out at the end of your day in the States, to find the CAD files waiting for you the next morning. Now everyone handles CAD in-house for the most part, but firms may still send out work that requires using state-of-the-art rendering or modeling technologies.

3. Nuts-and-bolts execution

A fair number of designers, especially high-profile, big-thinking ones, will have small aligned firms or executive architects who do, for lack of a better term, the nitty-gritty work for them. Some major, highly notable design firms have another firm do their working drawings, so the on-staff team can focus solely on design. When you are working outside of your own city, you may turn to a local firm or a local designer for on-the-ground, day-to-day assistance. This allows you to leverage yourself and build a relationship with someone who can support your work.

When you engage in relationships like these, you must be very careful to determine the scope of services and fees for the aligned firm and also ask for noncompete and confidentiality clauses to protect your relationship with your client.

4. Capabilities you'd like to offer clients but don't have expertise in

As your practice expands, you may find that there are disciplines that you'd like to eventually bring in-house—landscape architecture, say, or interior design, if you're an architect. Until you do, or even if you never have any intention of bringing them in-house, you can outsource these services. Firms typically take this approach when they want these services to be opaque to their clients. They want to offer a one-stop shop so that the client only has to deal with one entity, even though the work may be done by many.

A NOTE OF CAUTION ABOUT OUTSOURCING

It can save your firm time and money—and, certainly, head count—to have contracted individuals or teams of people outside of your office to do the sorts of work outlined above. It also can let you test the waters of a certain discipline or capability or technology without making a major commitment.

"Put the architect, interior designer, landscape designer, and contractor together as early as possible, so everybody feels that they are part of the team." CHRIS POLLACK

But there can be dangers to outsourcing. Every task or capability you outsource is a skill or set of skills that you're not building among your own team. For nondesign tasks, that's not such a big deal—you really don't need a CPA or controller or in-house publicist until you have a fairly large firm—but for design-related functions, you may be giving something up—quite possibly a lot. When you outsource, work gets done with less oversight from you, by people who may not know you and your firm well, and their interpretation of your aesthetic and your philosophy may not be exactly what you had in mind.

As you build your practice, you are also building a culture, as well as commitments among your staff and you and your firm. Outsourcing can compromise that culture and those commitments, which can sacrifice the long-term strength and stability of an organization. Your firm won't be as strong as it would be if you kept everything within the office.

The difference between hiring someone as a member of your staff and hiring someone as a consultant is the difference between creating shared intellectual property that belongs to your firm and being allowed to use someone else's work. This may seem like a subtle nuance, but it can affect not just what your firm produces but its entire culture. Paying an employee and training that employee means investing in the future of your firm, and it can pay dividends; cutting a consultant a check and providing some guidance is rarely more than exchanging money for services.

It's important to understand and recognize what you are giving away from your firm and taking away from your staff's ability to learn by outsourcing. Ultimately, if you want a full, well-rounded practice, you don't want to outsource too much or for too long.

Creating a Board of Advisors

A few years ago, I heard a story from one of my colleagues on the Leaders of Design Council that illustrates the power of building a small group of advisors who are committed to your success. One day, one of the long-term, high-net-worth clients of this designer—who, to an outside observer, would seem to have been quite successful—approached him and expressed some concern. "The way you run your business is just, well, an amazement to me," the client said. "We get invoices haphazardly, and communication between you and your clients isn't that strong. We love you, but your office is not functioning well."

This client, who ran a very strong business of his own, offered to step in, with a few other business-minded patron clients, to help the designer run his firm better. They started meeting with the designer on a quarterly basis to give him the skills he needed to successfully manage his firm. That group of clients became his panel of advisors, like a corporation's board of trustees. He brings them in to talk about business and management systems and growth opportunities, and his practice has been very successful, and much more organized, ever since.

Not every firm has to be as formal about it as this designer was, but you will certainly be stronger if you can find key people from both inside and outside the design industry whose strengths support your weaknesses and who can advise you on the big-picture questions, challenges, and opportunities of running your own firm. In fact, if the idea of a board of advisors doesn't quite appeal to you, you can get the same benefits and resources from a group of peers, with whom you get together on a regular basis to talk about what's happening in the profession. It's a healthy and helpful thing to have people who act as a sounding board, for discussions about all facets of your business.

BOARD OF ADVISORS BEST PRACTICES
Size

Four people should be sufficient, even for a very large firm. More than that on the panel can result in a too-many-cooks situation, with too many different and conflicting opinions. If you have fewer than fifteen staffers, you could probably have a board of just two.

Composition

Seek out people who are somewhat aligned but who also can offer various points of view. Select people from different business backgrounds, with different experiences, areas of expertise, and skills. You don't want adversarial relationships, exactly, but you do want to promote some healthy conflict, a bit of tension. Bringing in a bunch of people who'll just say yes to you and your ideas won't really help you. Ideally, you'll have:

- somebody who can sit back and listen to ideas

- somebody who can oppose ideas

- somebody who can support your ideas

- somebody who can generate ideas that will teach you how to move forward

This isn't to say that each member of your board should bring just one of these capabilities to the group; people can play very different roles in different situations. Ideally, each of them will be able to oppose you, to listen to you, to support you, or to teach you, depending on the question at hand. But, in reality, most people are skilled at two of these: an idea generator is usually also good at providing opposition to ideas, and the person who sits back and listens is usually also a good supporter of ideas.

Meetings

To make these advisory meetings productive you should meet at least quarterly. Meet in a space that is quiet and free from distractions—most likely not your office. Set an agenda and send it to each member in advance. You should list your desired outcomes from the meeting, and, most important, you should thank this group with a meal or other compensation (see the following page).

Compensation

In some cases, people will be willing to help you simply because they're friends or clients and they care about you and your business. In other cases, however, they may want some sort of remuneration. Some firms pay their advisors, but many will simply treat their boards to an all-expenses-paid retreat weekend at a great resort or even just a nice dinner with a wonderful bottle of wine. Still others may offer discounted or pro bono design services in exchange for the board members' time.

What Your Staff Should Say and Do to Support You in Front of Clients

As your firm expands in size, the individual members of your team will want to take on more responsibilities as they grow as designers. This is a positive thing, but it can also pose a challenge.

If your name is on the door, then clients have hired *you* as their designer, and they want to feel that all design directives and ideas are coming from *you,* not from junior, or maybe even senior, members of your staff. Understandably, this can frustrate your team, because they have ideas and opinions, too, and they want to feel that those matter, both to you and to the clients. They want to know that their point of view earns them respect.

But the client isn't really looking for just their individual advice. They're looking for—and, let's face it, paying for—the principal's point of view, so the client needs to feel that you're the one behind everything your staff suggest. Making the client feel that way is actually quite simple and really more about semantics than content. It all comes down to teaching your staff to speak in a certain way that supports you and the firm and makes the clients feel they're in safe hands. I think of it as: The Power of We.

> "Always use the collective 'we' with clients because it's not about you." **CHARLOTTE MOSS**

THE POWER OF WE

I always tell senior staff members that they will be far more successful in dealing with clients if they present ideas and solutions as coming directly from the firm's principal or, at the very least, born out of discussions with the principal. They should say things such as, "Keith and I think it would be a good idea if…" and "Keith and I were discussing, and…" Speaking this way may not immediately make your team members feel empowered, but it ultimately does give them strength and it allows them to be more effective in getting ideas across.

That's because there is great power in the "we" of "Keith and I," so much so that even principals of firms rarely say "I." They know that if they say "we," it implies that there's an entire team behind them and that the team has been diligently working away to find the best solutions to a project. Just saying "I" has none of this impact. Using "we" allows your staff to gain the confidence of their clients, and that, in turn, allows you as the firm's principal to relinquish some responsibilities and oversight. (Similarly, I always recommend bringing a member of your team to meetings, especially the first one you have with a potential client. When you show up with a senior member of your team who's going to handle the day-to-day work and be the client's primary contact, you're immediately setting the client's expectation that the relationship with your firm will involve other key members of your team. At the same time, you're signaling to the client that you trust the person you have brought with you and, by extension, your staff in general.)

At first, when a staffer is new or when you're starting to work with a new client, you'll only want the staffer to use the "we" sincerely and honestly, when you and the designer have actually discussed the aspect of the project being presented to a client. But once you know your designers understand what they're doing, you can release them to speak for you—always using the "we"—even if you haven't yet discussed a specific idea, decision, suggestion, or solution.

All that being said, the moment a client turns to a member of your team and directly asks for an opinion, that team member is free to give it—assuming, of course, that you're not in that meeting or on that call (if you are, then the designer should defer to you). Clients' asking for their opinion gives your team members permission to present their own thoughts. It tells your designers that the clients value their opinions and want to hear them.

I know explaining all of this to your staff might seem a bit patronizing or condescending, but it's your job to ask them to act this way—and, indeed, you are acting this way yourself—because it's the best way to get the firm's ideas across, to sell the client on the firm's designs, and to move a project forward. As part of a practice, you have to communicate in a way that represents that practice broadly.

Organizational Structures to Support Your Vision

The following organizational charts represent structures for firms of various sizes. The most efficient of these structures—the one I recommend you implement in your own firm—is the one based on the "studio system." What exactly is the studio system, you ask? It's a structure that lets you divide up your firm, no matter its size, into smaller and more manageable pods, or studios, each consisting of a lead person, most likely a studio director. Under the directors are usually project managers, and under them, midlevel staff, and under them, junior staff. A successful studio typically ranges between five and ten members. If a studio has more than ten members, it usually has a very strong leader and a very strong project manager.

Flat organizations, as shown in the middle chart opposite, can cause breakdowns in communication, while also putting a tremendous amount of pressure on the principal. The studio system, in contrast, allows for easy and open interaction and communication among people at various levels of hierarchy and skill. It also allows your firm to be nimble when taking on projects of different sizes. If one studio is swamped with work while another is waiting for a project to break, the latter can share staff members with the studio that requires help.

As you can see in the bottom chart, this studio system structure is also conducive to growth, as well as downsizing when necessary. **FIG 4.2**

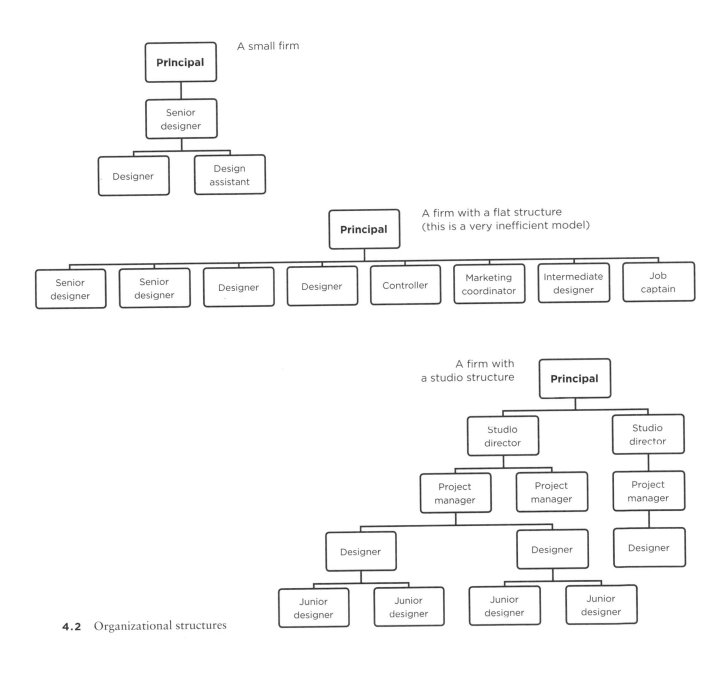

4.2 Organizational structures

Nurturing Your Team

Hiring the right people is one thing; holding on to them is quite another.

As the members of your team evolve and expand their skills, they'll look to take on new roles, tasks, and challenges. Their learning, growth, and development are as much *your* responsibility as theirs. As your firm's principal, you should be fully engaged in helping your staff to grow, giving them the support and the guidance they need to build a career at your studio, so they won't just see their position in your office as another job. You must cultivate your garden, as the saying goes.

TRAINING AND MENTORING

Training provides people with the skills they need to do the job that they were hired for, while mentoring gives them what they need to attain a future position that they and you envision. Training, then, is often more targeted and specific, while mentoring is more holistic and general.

Training

Training starts off in a fairly straightforward way. The members of your staff who directly manage recent hires need to teach these newbies how to do their jobs—and, just as important, how to do so within your firm's culture and your way of getting things done. New hires' colleagues at the same level can also play a role in this, with an established junior designer on one team, for example, showing the ropes to a newly hired junior designer on another team.

Key in the training process is allowing errors to happen. Errors, followed by immediate (gentle) corrections and (constructive) criticism, help people learn and grow. If people aren't given space in which to make mistakes and to learn from those mistakes, they're not going to improve. Of course, if a new hire just keeps making the same or similar mistakes again and again and proves that he or she isn't learning from these errors, then you will need to let that person go, ideally at the end of the ninety-day review period.

As employees get more and more sophisticated, they may seek out (or you may seek out for them) types of training that they can't receive from other members of your staff. When training is not available internally, you'll need to find local classes or workshops. This doesn't all fall on you, however. You should ask your employees who want to gain additional skills to find ways to acquire them, and then you can fund, or help fund, these studies, as long as the coursework is aligned with your needs and goals and not just those of the employee.

It seems like a lot of work, and it can be exhausting—especially if it's exhaustive—but if you train the right people to do the right jobs, you will have a much more productive team, full of employees who are continually taking on more responsibility and becoming more accountable for their work.

Mentoring

Mentoring goes much deeper and extends over a much longer period of time. It's about achieving goals that are further in the future.

For you to mentor someone well, the two of you need to be aligned about goals. Then you have to engage on a regular basis so that you can deliver information and check on the employee's progress. Just like in school, everyone needs assignments, and someone needs to evaluate the progress of those assignments. We suggest to our clients who are looking to implement a mentoring program that they assign to each new employee a buddy with a great deal of expertise and experience that align with the growth objectives of the recent hire. This buddy then becomes the person to make and check in on assignments, while also generally guiding the new person through the firm.

Some examples of assignments to help mentor new staff members might be:

- researching new building codes and then communicating their findings to the rest of the staff;

- researching new resources for product development and finding more rarefied artisans to keep your company innovative;

- visiting a job site and reporting back on the quality of the craftsmanship to make certain it matches the design expectations.

If you simply have a sink-or-swim mentality, then some people will grow because they are entrepreneurial and self-starters, but the ones who need more (but could well be future rock stars) may just sink. And even your entrepreneurial self-starters can get frustrated if they feel no one is paying attention to them. You need to judge each person's growth needs individually and then differentiate the services and guidance you provide.

Mentoring takes many forms: It comes from working closely with the people you manage, sometimes just rolling up a chair next to them and seeing what they're working on or showing them some different ways of doing things. It may mean bringing them to a job site or a client meeting, so they gain understanding of working in the field. It can involve outside coursework and training beyond the office. Ultimately, though, it all comes down to paying attention—to them, to their work, to their goals—to make sure your staff feels that you're invested in their future.

Paying attention to your high performers—the folks who seem as though they can operate without any oversight or guidance from you—is just as, if not more, important than paying attention to the people who obviously need your help and support. The people in your firm who cry out for help will always get help, but that can leave your most competent people feeling ignored. They may then be much more willing to jump ship when another opportunity comes along—and they're the last people you want to lose.

Please check out the delegation chart in Chapter Four of *The Business of Design* for additional information on the process of bringing up to speed and mentoring your employees.

INSPIRING GROWTH BY SETTING GOALS AND REVIEWING PERFORMANCE

To set your staff up for long-term success, you need to work with them to establish goals, develop a road map for reaching those goals, and then review their progress toward them. That's how you inspire them to grow—and the growth of your firm is very much tied up in your employees' individual professional growth.

Setting goals

It's human nature for people to wonder what their future will look like. So it's essential to map that out for employees. In the beginning, goals may just be about growing from one position to the next. To help employees create a road map to that goal, you can show them what the step-by-step evolution of their career at your firm could look like—what it takes to go from being a junior designer to being a project manager or from project manager to senior designer. This means showing them the job descriptions for these future roles and then determining what skills they will need to reach those goals and how the firm will help them to acquire those skills. For instance, if a move from junior designer to project manager requires more experience on job sites, then you and the employee will discuss sending that staffer on site more.

Especially today—with a generation of millennial employees who want you to communicate as much as possible and who exist in a need-to-know mode about their future—establishing these goals and maps is valuable. Millennials want to know that everything they're doing has purpose. Addressing this and helping them understand their value within your firm is your responsibility.

Reviewing performance

Helping your employees establish their goals and understand how they can achieve them through training and mentoring is just the beginning. You also will need to check in with them to review their progress and make sure they're still on track.

It's important to formally review your staff annually, of course, but it's just as important to make sure you have some sort of system in place to touch base with them throughout the year, to see how they're doing not only with the work in their current role, but also with longer-term, bigger-picture goals. This can be as simple as scheduling fifteen-minute chats once a quarter between employees and managers to make sure that employees are meeting their goals and receiving support from their managers. Open communication goes a long way toward helping your staff grow.

More formal reviews should happen once a year, often in December or January, though some firms will spread their reviews out over the course of the entire year. (I personally like to stagger mine, doing reviews at the anniversary of an employee's hiring date.) They should usually last about one to two hours, depending on how many goals you need to set; the employee to be reviewed should be joined by a staff member who reports directly to that person and a senior member of your staff. These meetings should cover the employee's development over the last year and goals for the next twelve months, as well as what he or she has received and requires from management. (Note that it isn't necessary for the principal, especially at a larger firm, to attend every review meeting.)

Prior to the meeting you should complete a review form. This form should be used to discuss the employee's progress together at the review. It will help you to evaluate the employee and will also be used to set goals for the coming year. **FIG 4.3**

The primary purpose of staff reviews is to make certain your employees understand exactly what will be expected of them during the coming year and, equally

🌲 **Redwood Design Group**

Employee Performance Review

Date

Name	Employee ID

Job title	Review period

Department	Manager

1 = POOR 2 = FAIR 3 = SATISFACTORY 4 = GOOD 5 = EXCELLENT

Knowledge of job
1 ○ 2 ○ 3 ○ 4 ○ 5 ○

COMMENTS

Quality of work
1 ○ 2 ○ 3 ○ 4 ○ 5 ○

COMMENTS

Ability to think independently
1 ○ 2 ○ 3 ○ 4 ○ 5 ○

COMMENTS

Takes initiative
1 ○ 2 ○ 3 ○ 4 ○ 5 ○

COMMENTS

Communication/listening skills
1 ○ 2 ○ 3 ○ 4 ○ 5 ○

COMMENTS

Reliability
1 ○ 2 ○ 3 ○ 4 ○ 5 ○

COMMENTS

Overall rating
1 ○ 2 ○ 3 ○ 4 ○ 5 ○

COMMENTS

ADDITIONAL COMMENTS

GOALS FOR COMING YEAR (AS AGREED UPON BY EMPLOYEE AND MANAGER)

Employee signature	Date

Manager signature	Date

BY SIGNING THIS FORM, YOU CONFIRM THAT YOU HAVE DISCUSSED THIS REVIEW IN DETAIL WITH YOUR SUPERVISOR.
SIGNING THIS FORM DOES NOT NECESSARILY INDICATE THAT YOU AGREE WITH THIS EVALUATION.

4.3 Sample review form

important, what they can expect from you. Reviews exist to ensure that your staff is on the right path to achieve success.

As you may have noticed, reviews should be about goal setting, not about course correction. If a problem arises with an employee's performance, that needs to be addressed and worked through immediately. You should not wait for an annual or even a quarterly review to bring it up. Reviews are not for punitive actions or airings of grievances, either yours or your employees'.

I also believe that annual reviews shouldn't be about salary. If employees know that their reviews will conclude with an announcement about a raise or a bonus, your staffers will spend the entire meeting wondering about those numbers and will be distracted from engaging in the review. I find it best to make annual reviews concerned only with goals and performance and then to do a salary review a few weeks later. This allows you to use information gleaned from the annual review in your salary calculations.

ACCOUNTABILITY: YOURS AND THEIRS

A big piece of nurturing your team comes down to the agreement you make with your staff—tacit or otherwise—that you are going to help them grow as individuals and that they, in turn, are going to help your firm grow. You've made a pact that you are all going to support one another in these efforts, and it's vital that everyone remains accountable to this promise.

But how do you do that? The main way is to follow through on all you've said you'll do for your employees: helping them set goals and develop a path to achieving them, mentoring and training them, and then rewarding them when they've developed the skills they need to grow into the role they have set as their goal. Your role in the accountability equation is to show people how they can advance and then to follow through by moving them up a rung on the ladder, demonstrating that you're willing to give them new authority. (For goals that aren't just about a new role, there may be other incentives, such as salary increases, bonuses, or spot rewards, such as, say, a special Monday off after a hellish week spent getting a project out the door by Friday.) Employees' living up to their end of the bargain is just as key. They need to show their accountability by developing the skills and earning the responsibility that a promotion requires.

In conclusion, building the right team is the most significant capital you will create for your organization. Finding good people, nurturing these people, and growing together to build a career and not just a job is what will make your firm an everlasting successful business for you and your team.

Design is as much about execution as it is about talent, and what is required to execute your designs is a strong team. Keep your eye on your team—keep them challenged, engaged, fulfilled, and rewarded—and your own rewards will be plentiful.

CHAPTER FIVE

The People You *Don't* Need in Your Life

EVEN THOUGH THIS CHAPTER is called "The People You *Don't* Need in Your Life," it is really about honoring all the people you do deserve to have in your life. In the professional service industry, where people are our greatest asset, building the right team is everything. This chapter is about supporting your team by weeding out toxic clients, bad employees, and other people who are simply not right for your organization. While it may seem terribly negative to talk about the people you don't need, this chapter is quite possibly the most important one of this entire book. It is not always easy to recognize the early warning signs of **difficult people**; these pages will guide you in spotting them before you enter too far into relationships with them.

A couple of years ago I was working with a client who has a twenty-person firm and is probably one of the top ten nicest people I know. We were in a staff meeting, and it occurred to me that as nice as he was, his staff was not. There was an entire group of "mean girls" who were making the office a very unpleasant place to work; it truly felt like high school. These employees were never happy with anything they were asked to do. They hated new members of the company and found a way to alienate anyone who tried to break up their posse. After the meeting I spoke with my client. My words were few, but they were powerful: "You deserve better than this." Perplexed, he asked what I was talking about. I slowly identified each of these employees and why they were the wrong fit for his office. Two people proved to be the ringleaders; they literally bullied the others into following their lead. At this particular time they had decided they hated a new senior designer who had just joined the firm. Rather than helping him acclimate to the office, they created roadblocks every step of the way and reported every mistake he made. The firm's work was suffering because so much time was spent hating the designer that no one was paying attention to what was not getting done.

The transformation was immediate. My client let some people go, and others who had been stuck under the thumbs of the bullies turned their attitude around quickly. Today the office is much more efficient and successful, and it truly has a pleasant environment. It is important never to underestimate the power of a small group or even a powerful individual to influence the culture of your company; this is why it is so important to hire carefully for the right people with the right fit. I believe that if my client had really been paying attention to fit, these "mean girls" would never have been hired.

Now we'll look at all the types of people you don't need in your life, whether clients, employees, or colleagues.

Toxic Clients

Let's start with clients—or shall I say, bad clients.

Let me qualify this by saying there is a difference between difficult and bad clients. Difficult clients are not a rare thing. Few people get to a place where they can afford to hire a designer without being somewhat demanding and difficult. Difficult is actually not the issue; the issue is clients whom you do not trust. The most essential ingredient of a good relationship is trust. Most disputes come from a lack of trust and a lack of communication skills. It may sound like a cliché, but trust must be earned, and you need to fill up your trust bank account in order to successfully navigate difficult situations.

When you first work with a client, the slate is pretty clean. You can form a deep relationship in which trust builds quickly or you can have a standoffish client who takes time to trust you and let you in. These are both acceptable situations; the clients to look out for are the ones who come into the relationship with a preconceived notion that they trust no one. They tend to be very negative people and tend to not respect your talents.

Trust your gut. If something does not feel right about a potential client, most likely it is not right.

TOP TEN WARNING SIGNS OF TOXIC CLIENTS

1. They don't offer you a glass of water.

It may seem flip to think that clients who don't offer you a glass of water are not good clients, but trust me, it signals that clients aren't thinking of anybody but themselves.

2. They don't ask you anything about yourself.

You are about to spend a great deal of time over several months—maybe years— together, and if they don't seem interested in you or your work, the relationship is sure to be strained. They need to understand you as much as you need to understand them; that is the basic ground rule for effective communication.

3. They don't tell you anything about themselves.

If it is difficult to get clients to open up about who they are and how they live or work, then designing their project will be very difficult. If they are coming to you for *your design*, then they are buying a product from you. But if they are coming to you to help them articulate *their design*, you will need to know who they are and how they function.

4. They tell you that they make quick decisions.

The only clients who ever say this are the ones who have been told that they can't make a decision or that they are difficult to work with. It is a huge red flag. You will decide for yourself whether they can make quick decisions. If they can't, your project could be very costly and drag on much longer than anticipated.

5. They tell you that they are easy to work with.

See number four. If they tell you they are easy to work with, it is usually because they have been told that they are difficult and they are trying to sell you on working for them. Again, only you will be able to tell whether they are easy to work with, once you have started their project.

6. They promise you future work if you discount your current fees.

If designers made this sort of deal every time a client proposed it, we would all go broke. It is a typical strategy for developers or homeowners who have multiple projects. The truth, however, is that the most time-consuming projects are the first ones because it takes time to understand a client. I recommend that my clients reverse this offer. Say, "I am happy to talk about discounts for multiple projects. Let's finish the first one, and if all goes well, we would certainly consider a price reduction on the next one, if that makes sense for the project." Remember, however, that projects are not prototypes; each one tends to be unique, and if you agree ahead of time to discount the second one and it is completely different from the first, you risk losing money on that project. Economy of scale comes only from efficiency and understanding your client better on the next project. If Vincent van Gogh had painted a picture for clients and they asked for a second one, would that one be worth any less? You may not be van Gogh, but your value is your value. But also remember that just the fact that a client has asked for a discount doesn't mean you should turn down the project; it is simply a warning sign that you may be asked for a deal project after project and you will need to make sure the client understands your value.

7. You are their third designer.

This is such a personal profession that it is not a good sign if clients burn through designers. Of course, if there is a reasonable explanation for their having worked with multiple designers, it is worth understanding, but chances are these clients are difficult people.

8. You don't get to meet them.

In today's world, some clients are surrounded by a battery of handlers. I have experienced cases in which a client lets handlers manage the entire project. This may not be an issue for a commercial project, but for a residential project, it is almost impossible to design for an absentee owner.

9. Only half of them show up to meetings.

When you work with a couple, the person you meet may not be the one writing the checks. Too often a designer can be led down a path that matches the expectation of one partner, and then when the other one shows up, he or she doesn't agree with the direction or the budget, and the project needs to be redesigned. Make sure both parties attend all major decision-making meetings.

10. They have chronic amnesia.

If clients constantly can't remember that they approved an idea or design or if they forget to make payments, these are signs you are dealing with bad clients.

Each of these warnings signs is significant, but they are not the only reasons to say no. They are merely warning signs, and you will need to dig deeper to understand whether this client will be too difficult to work with.

THE FEAR OF SAYING NO

We often fear that if we say no to a project, no matter how wrong it may feel, we may be saying no to the last client who will ever walk through our door. A close runner-up to this is the fear that the project we turn away could have been our best, offering a commission that would have turned into something major—an amazing opportunity that we'd kick ourselves for passing up. Connected to that is the idea that a potential commission could create a patron client for your firm, someone who would turn to you again and again for various homes and offices, and that if you say no, all that work would wind up in the hands of your competition.

You could be right about any of these scenarios, but if your gut and your head tell you that this person could be a big problem, then you're liable to be in much worse shape if you take this client on than you would be by losing some of that business. (And, believe me, that client is definitely not the last one who'll ever walk through your door.)

Saying no is the most powerful thing you can do as a designer. It means you are confident about whom you want to work with and whom you want in your life. It is being respectful of your needs and not beholden to your fears.

WHEN YOU SAY YES TO THE WRONG CLIENT

The results of saying yes to the wrong client can be far more damaging than just dealing with a difficult personality; the effects can be widespread and far-reaching. Here are a few examples:

- You are focused on the demands of this client, and they take you away from easier clients who deserve equal attention.

- Your staff resents the fact that they have to deal with unreasonable people, and they start resenting their jobs, maybe even resenting you. This can ultimately lead to their leaving your firm.

- The vendors, contractors, or consultants whom you have directed to this client may begin to question your judgment.

- The client will never be satisfied. He or she will talk poorly about you in public, and your reputation could suffer. That being said, many people will understand the source, and when this difficult person starts complaining about you and your firm, the grievances may not have that much credence. But these negative comments are still harmful if circulating or being posted online.

- Lastly, a client like this is usually a very unhappy person who will not be not satisfied until everyone else is just as unhappy. You don't want or need that bad energy in your life.

A client of mine once began working with a client who had a huge team of handlers, and all decisions came through the filter of those handlers. There was no personal relationship with the client himself and no indication what he liked or hated. The problem arose when, after a tremendous amount of work, the designer received feedback that the client was very unhappy with his selections. He was asked to re-create the presentation with little feedback other than that the client did not like it, but it is impossible to work in a bubble and simply guess the likes or dislikes of your client. The warning signs had all been there that the client was bad because he had not been available during the negotiation talks and the designer had never heard firsthand his vision for the project.

In another case, a client designed a home for a married couple who would never come to a single meeting together. My client knew this was trouble because the person writing the checks never was available to sign off on the designs and allow the project to move forward. The designer should have listened to her gut and turned away the job, but she really liked the wife, who had told her that the project was her passion. The designer didn't learn until it was too late that even though it was the wife's passion, the husband (who controlled the purse strings) had never agreed to it. The project was never finished, and the clients were left unhappy. The miscommunication between the couple was so bad that they wound up getting a divorce at the end of the project.

TEACHING A BAD CLIENT TO BECOME A GOOD CLIENT

On rare occasions, even when you are hired by a bad client, you may have an opportunity to turn things around. Sometimes it all comes down to educating the client. If a client really doesn't know how to work with a designer, expectations of how to treat the designer and of how to build the relationship can be far off the mark. It will be your job to clear this up and build a more realistic framework for your interactions. I once had a client who bordered on abusive, and I waited until I could no longer stand his tone or

> "The most difficult clients usually come with the best potential projects, and that's an opportunity for career growth." MARC SZAFRAN

The Wrong Employee

While taking on a bad client has a finite impact on your business—though not as finite as you might have thought before reading the previous section—taking on a bad employee can be even more damaging to your business. As with clients, sometimes issues with an employee don't surface immediately. Again I want to emphasize: hire slowly and, above all, seek people with a good cultural fit, and you will be less likely to pick bad employees. **FIG 5.1**

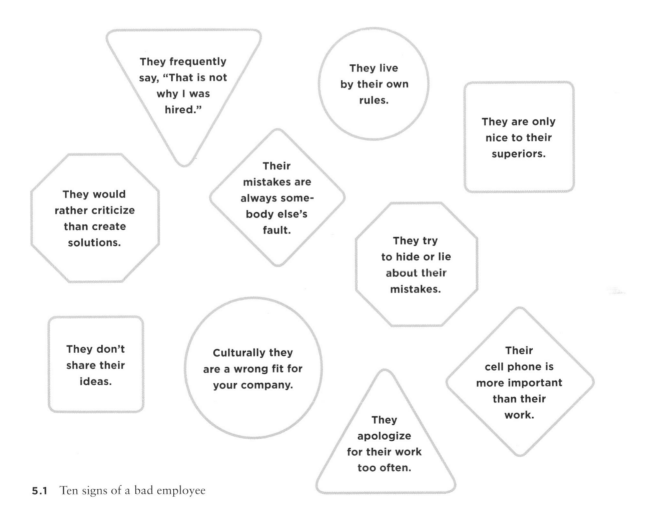

5.1 Ten signs of a bad employee

THE WARNING SIGNS

Let's start from the beginning: the day you first interviewed this employee. Did everything seem right, or were you ignoring warning signs? Maybe his résumé did not match his portfolio or how he seemed in person. Perhaps he didn't show up on time for the interview and then made excuses? Were there discrepancies in the story he told about his life, education, and career that were evident in either his résumé or what he said in the interview? Did he seem confident in his abilities? Or was he just a little on edge and uneasy when speaking about his skills?

One of my clients asks candidates to eat lunch with his entire office after the initial screening. He will not hire anyone before his staff has had a chance to meet with the candidates and observe how they handle themselves during this lunch. This allows all the members of the office to feel as though their insights are valuable.

There are numerous warning signs that you can look for during the interview process; here are my top ten:

- **A résumé that doesn't add up** Dates are missing, the timeline is off, or there are too many gaps between jobs. Is there overlap with the dates between jobs? Be aware of inconsistencies.

- **A lack of attention to appearance** It is always better to be over-dressed for an interview. If someone comes in a suit and your office is more casual, you can explain that your office is informal but you appreciate the candidate's dressing up for the interview.

- **Difficulty communicating** The candidate fumbles when talking about past experience and qualifications. You want employees who can be articulate and speak with confidence. They're going to be representing you in front of clients.

> "Be slow to hire and always hold the last interview at a restaurant. Talking over a meal tells you a lot about a person."
> **SUZANNE TUCKER**

- **Overconfidence** The candidate is bombastic about past roles, and expectations of responsibility don't match experience.

- **Put-downs** The candidate speaks poorly about others, especially past employers.

- **Hyperawareness or overpreparedness** A candidate knows an almost creepy amount about you or your firm and obviously has been digging to find personal information that makes you uncomfortable, for example, where your kids go to school or where your spouse works. If someone discovers a connection with you during the interview that helps to establish common ground, that is OK. But it is never acceptable for a person to Google you to create an artificial connection.

- **A questionable online trail** When you Google or look up a candidate on social media sites, you find that too much personal information is available. Before making the hire, consider what clients would think if they discovered this about a person on their team.

- **Money talk** The candidate asks for compensation, concessions, benefits, or time off before being offered the position. Recently we had a candidate ask for stock options on a privately held company during the interview. Their potential role did not even warrant that kind of discussion, and it was a complete turnoff.

- **Lateness** A candidate is late for the interview without good reason. Traffic is not a valid excuse, nor is leaving a previous appointment late. Timeliness says a lot about planning skills.

- **Plagiarism** The person's portfolio is filled with others' work. Sometimes it is difficult to know, but the design community is small, and often you will recognize work you have already seen in print or elsewhere.

It should be clear that not all of these warning signs are deal breakers. If a candidate is late once, it is fairly easy to excuse that behavior. But if a candidate presents a plagiarized portfolio, that is a definite no.

THE EFFECTS OF BAD EMPLOYEES

A bad seed may do a remarkably good job of hiding his worst characteristics during interviews, and you may not realize you've made a mistake until the new employee starts working for you. Then what do you do?

In Chapter Four, I included a chart that will help you to evaluate your employees' skill level and their fit within your firm's culture.

As I explained in that chapter, if you only hire people with a high skill level, with little or no concern for how their personalities will mesh with your firm and your staff, you run the risk of those people being cultural misfits. This is much more likely to bring a firm down than is a lack of skill.

When firms bring in what we call "competent jerks," they always lose employees, and not just any employees—they lose the good ones. We all know competent jerks; they are highly skilled but could not care less about being liked. That makes it hard for everyone who works with them, but especially the people they manage. It is usually very obvious when someone is a competent jerk, but the really skilled ones know how to work the system so that only those beneath them on the org chart feel the pain. People like this can seem entirely likable to their principal or supervisor, but to their peers and subordinates they are a nightmare. Competent jerks are very manipulative, and they cannot be trusted.

> "Recognize that every part of your firm that touches the public—what your lobby looks like, how clients are greeted—is part of your marketing plan." MEG TOUBORG

As the story about the office "mean girls" at the beginning of this chapter illustrates, a bad employee, or, even worse, a powerful clique of bad employees, can affect your firm in very dangerous ways. A few years ago, I had a client who refused to believe that one of his employees was poisoning the culture of his company. For instance, the firm had a no-jeans policy, and he was the only one allowed to wear jeans. If you have different rules for certain privileged employees, then you are headed for a significant number of disgruntled people. My client was extremely busy and needed this person to run the office while he was meeting with clients and designing major lines of products. Despite continued gripes from the staff about this individual and all kinds of warning signs—not least of all a long-term, trusted employee's resignation—my client chose to turn a blind eye to the situation. Eventually, but not before serious damage had been done, the bad employee revealed his true self to my client, who then fired him for insubordination. My client finally recognized all the bad habits of this employee only through reading his email exchanges with others; this particular person had not even made the effort to cover his tracks.

One of my favorite quotes, from Maya Angelou, is "When people show you who they are, believe them the first time." My client above should have kept that in mind. The best leaders have a sixth sense about what makes their staff tick. If you are the principal of your firm, you need to develop the skill of quickly assessing people and keeping track of anyone who may seem not quite right for your firm.

Here are a few ways in which poisonous employees can bring you and your firm down:

- They are divisive, alienating your loyal staffers while attracting and cultivating those who will follow them.

- Similarly, they disrupt the culture you've worked to create in order to try to build their own.

- They provoke valuable staff members to quit.

- They tend to be untrustworthy, and this breeds an environment that is less trusting.

- They prey on people's weaknesses rather than cultivating their strengths, believing if others look weaker, they will look stronger. A skilled leader supports people's strengths and helps them overcome their weaknesses.

- They make other employees wonder why you keep such a terrible person on staff—does that person know something about you? Are you secretly that bad, too, or do you just have poor judgment?

- Poisonous people don't affect only your staff; they also can destroy relationships with clients. If a client asks for a particular person to be removed from a project, this is a major warning sign.

HOW TO TURN A BAD EMPLOYEE INTO A GOOD EMPLOYEE

It is never easy to change people, but there are instances when you can retrain a bad employee to become an asset to your firm. It is often easier to change employees from bad to good than it is to change clients; employees typically will try to do anything to keep their jobs.

That being said, some employees simply don't care whether they are liked. But this is unusual—and hopefully your interview process will weed these people out. Generally no one comes into a business to be mean and divisive. These are usually learned behaviors that, for whatever reason, have worked for people in the past at other firms and in other studios.

Sometimes bad behavior is simply the result of bad experiences, bad examples, bad habits, or even just different ways of doing things picked up from previous employers. In one firm it may be acceptable to arrive late to meetings, and in another it may be acceptable to speak poorly of your peers. Younger employees tend to come with less of this type of baggage, so they may require less drastic effort to change their bad behavior. If you lay down the ground rules for acceptable behavior at your firm, you can attempt to fix those learned behaviors.

For example, if someone comes from an office where everyone yells, there will need to be an adjustment to make sure that behavior doesn't carry into your firm. You will need to address bad behaviors on a case-by-case basis, as soon as you are aware of them, and redirect your employee to more acceptable behavior. You can accomplish this through mentoring; remember that mentoring is as much about conveying culture as it is about teaching skills. It is your job as a principal to show what you expect of employees, from skills to cultural fit.

Years ago one of my clients hired a very talented young designer. She was incredibly skilled at creating renderings, and she knew it, as did everyone at the firm. But this employee was extremely stubborn and a terrible communicator. She had a "my way or the highway" attitude, which came from her limited experience dealing directly with clients and employees. If anyone needed changes or suggested improvements to anything she drew, she angrily lashed out. As a result, her colleagues started looking for alternative resources for their renderings, such as outside services or other talented people in their office. When she finally realized that her job was in jeopardy because fewer and fewer people were taking advantage of her unique skills, she herself reached out to the firm's principals for help. In the end she did change her ways of dealing with people, and everyone is now working more in harmony than ever.

Sometimes all it takes to work through a problem is to let employees see that their own behavior is causing the problems they are facing and that if they change that behavior, the problems will disappear. But more often than not, unfortunately, the employee has no interest in changing or may not be capable of it—the behavior may just be ingrained in who they are. These employees need to either move on to a firm that can accept their behavior or become a consultant so they will not be required to be part of anyone else's culture.

HOW TO FIRE A BAD EMPLOYEE

I once had a client say to me, "I wish letting go of people would get easier or that I would become better at it." I responded that I didn't think she would ever want to be that hardened person who is good at firing people.

If you do need to remove a bad employee, make sure to do your homework. Document what has led up to the firing. Even though most of us live in a state with at-will employment, it is not always that easy to fire someone. You typically need to put people on probation or warn them that their behavior or work is not up to your expectations. Word your remarks carefully and be cautious about saying anything that can be interpreted as a disparaging comment.

Firms often have a difficult time telling employees why they are being let go. I am a firm believer in honesty and straightforwardness. If you sugarcoat the reasons you are laying someone off, it is confusing and can send mixed messages to your vendors, other designers, and showrooms. Be clear and concise and state your case.

The Rest of the World That You Don't Need

Through the years I have learned that surrounding myself with only the people I want to be with is what makes me happy, successful, and fulfilled. That sense of whom I *do* want around me has very much informed my understanding of whom I *don't* want.

That means avoiding people who are just out for themselves. Any professional service firm must be collaborative; it's an innate trait of the field. That's why this whole book is, ultimately, about collaboration.

There are certain common types of potential collaborators, colleagues, or contractors/vendors who don't care about you:

- the recruiter who is out for the best fees and will poach from your firm despite being your client

- the craftsperson who produces a unique item that you have designed for your client and then sells it to others without your permission

- the employee who moonlights

- the consultant who gives away your intellectual property to other clients

- the client who goes behind your back to purchase directly from your sources

- the vendor who couldn't care less about servicing you

- the tennis pro who sleeps with your spouse (just making sure you are reading this!)

All of the people listed above have one thing in common: they only care about themselves. As this book emphasizes: *surround yourself with like-minded people.*

I ask you simply to pay attention and stay alert to the people around you. I believe strongly in community, in collaboration, and in human decency. Be aware of those who will not serve you well and stay away from them. There should be a high level of respect in all your relationships, because without respect people are not kind to each other. There are plenty of good people in the world. Keep your focus on them.

CHAPTER SIX

The Things Only You Can Do

THE GREAT ARTS EDUCATION PHILOSOPHER Maxine Greene once said, "You cannot experience wonder until you can learn to live without answers and live with ambiguity." Part of your job as a creative is to explore the unexplored. To do this you need to have the room in your life to allow for your creativity and you need to surround yourself with people who enable you to focus on your strengths by doing all the things that you are not as good at. These people will provide the space for **ambiguity** to live in your creative mind and will make room for the **wonder** you need to explore your creativity. Both these elements will expand your mind, feed your soul, and give great energy to your talents.

In the spirit of Greene's thinking: at a retreat for one of my clients, people were sharing stories of how they avoid exposing their shortcomings or weaknesses to their staff in fear of being "found out" as someone who doesn't know everything. Well, none of us knows everything (except maybe my brother Craig, who has an encyclopedic memory). A light bulb went off for me as I was observing their discussion. I began to recognize how this fear of being exposed holds us back and limits our ability to learn.

Fear is a weakness; vulnerability is a strength.

If we operate out of fear, we don't communicate well. We close ourselves off from our ability to be self-critical and to analyze ourselves for self-improvement, and therefore we stop growing. If we allow ourselves to become vulnerable to new ideas, then sharing and learning from others will provide for greater growth. Some people may think that vulnerability is a weakness because it means that people could take advantage of you—it means

"Recognize that no one is perfect, that the magic is when a bunch of imperfect people do something amazing together." **MARK FERGUSON**

that you are exposed in some way. But when have you ever truly learned when you did not expose yourself? Years ago I had a client who told me that as a principal of his firm, he felt as if he were the only person who did not have the opportunity to grow within his firm's structure. I immediately challenged him because if we stop growing, we stop being relevant, and in a creative world it is imperative that we remain relevant. (And the truth is, that particular client has grown leaps and bounds from that day almost twenty years ago.)

Why We Need People

Simon Sinek has said, "If we were good at everything we'd have no need for each other." It is a misconception that a true leader has to excel at everything; good leaders know what they are not good at and recognize their weaknesses. A great leader knows a little about a lot of things and allows each team member to become highly skilled in an area of expertise. The job of a great leader is to point and not to judge: show people the way, then allow them to do their job.

I learned this lesson at my first job at Gensler. Art Gensler was a master at hiring strong people. He was a brilliant businessman but would be the first to tell you that he was not the most talented designer. An architect needs many skills, and design is only one of them. He surrounded himself with the best talent in the industry and grew his company into the largest architectural firm in the world.

Your Work Life Is an Onion

My friend Beth Farb shared this analogy with me: if your work life is an onion, each layer represents a task or responsibility. Your goal is to peel your way to the core by removing all the layers that someone else could handle better. One layer, for example, may be financial management. If you are a creative person, this might not be your strength; therefore you should peel that layer off and hand it to a bookkeeper,

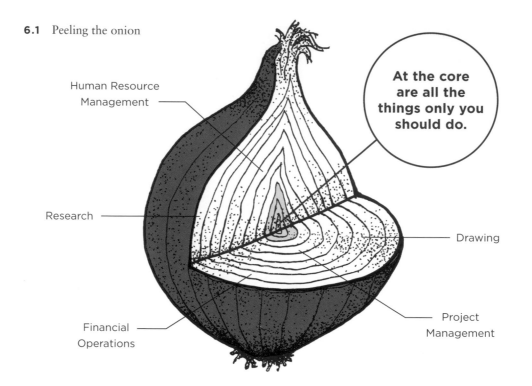

6.1 Peeling the onion

Human Resource Management

Research

Financial Operations

At the core are all the things only you should do.

Drawing

Project Management

controller, or CFO. Another example might be project management: really getting into your projects may not be the best use of your time. In the end, the layers that remain are your core skills—the work you truly enjoy. **FIG 6.1**

One client of mine probably has the most fulfilling job of anyone I know. He has narrowed down the thing he is best at and has mastered the art of allowing others in his organization to handle everything else. He is the lead architect for most of his projects; after he conceives the designs he hands them off to his skilled team to be executed. My client spent years nurturing the right team so that their skills complemented each other to produce beautiful work. He loves his job because he gets to do what he loves and nothing less. One day he commented to me that he was "the least unhappy person" he knew. That is truly what each of us deserves to feel.

> "Have a vision for your work to make it easier for people to identify you with a certain kind of task." **GIL SCHAFER**

FINDING YOUR STRENGTHS AND WEAKNESSES

So let's start with how to understand your strengths and weaknesses, as well as what you don't know. The exercise is simple and will help you to evaluate where you would like to be spending more or less of your time. It takes no real effort to identify your strengths and weaknesses, if you are honest with yourself. And yet it is difficult because we are not always the best judge of our own talents. **FIG 6.2**

Start by listing what you absolutely love to do and work your way down to the things you wish you did not have to do. Then rank that list of activities in order of how skilled you feel you are at each—not considering whether you love doing them or not, but rather prioritizing those that truly belong on your plate because they are your highest and best use. Make a copy of your list, removing your ranking, and share it with the person you are most connected to and who knows you the

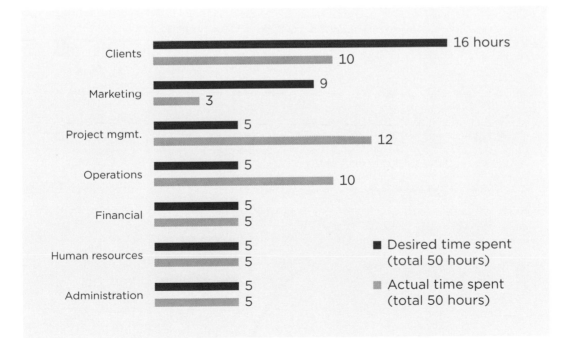

6.2 A sample graph showing a principal's actual versus desired time spent on various activities

best. Ask this person also to rank your tasks in terms of your level of skill at each. Compare the two lists; see whether you agree with your trusted partner about the activities you are best at and the ones that you might need to delegate.

ASSESSING YOUR SKILLS AND TALENTS

Ranking your strengths and weaknesses:

- Start with absolutely all the things you do. It doesn't matter whether you are the right person to do those tasks. For example, you may love to make your own travel arrangements—it may not be the best use of your time, but you enjoy doing it.

- Once you have covered all the things you do, then check the things on this list that you know only you can do. The list should begin to get shorter.

- Now rank the checked items in order of how important they are to your work.

- Now mark all those things that you wish someone would take off your plate.

- From that list think carefully about the things that you know only you should do, even though they are not your favorite things.

- Finally, make a list of the things that someone else can do; figure out what skill sets are needed so that you may delegate those things. **FIG 6.3**

THE BUSINESS OF CREATIVITY

ASSESSING YOUR SKILLS

Tasks to be done:	By me	With senior designers	By others
Meeting potential clients		✓	
Reviewing financials	✓		
Interviews for publications	✓		
Reviewing drawings			✓
Junior staff reviews			✓
Making travel arrangements			✓
Meet with accountant	✓		
Strategic planning	✓		
Project selections	✓		
Writing proposals			✓

6.3 A sample list of responsibilities to keep and those to give away

Now let's further explore how to analyze your strengths and weaknesses as tools for growth:

- Visualize your strengths and weaknesses on a graph, with the y-axis identifying strengths and weaknesses and the x-axis listing all your tasks. This visual will give you a good perspective on how balanced your work life might be and which tasks may need to be delegated in order to create a more fulfilling career. There is a reason why your strengths belong to you. Most likely, not only are you good at them but you also enjoy doing them as well. When we do the things we love we do them with passion, pride, and joy.

- Once you understand your weaknesses you will have two choices. You can find the right people to do the tasks that you have identified as your weaknesses. Or, you can figure out whether you are interested in obtaining those skills for yourself to build these weaknesses into strengths.

    I used to struggle to find the confidence to make presentations. I was always able to create good conversation on a one-on-one basis, but I was never great at speaking in front of a crowd. I decided I could obtain this skill by teaching, so I committed to UCLA's Extension Architecture and Interior Design Program as a teacher and guest lecturer. After seventeen years of lecturing, public speaking with large and small groups alike is very comfortable for me.

- Focus on building a support structure to delegate the things that someone else should be doing. If you surround yourself with strong people, then they will make you stronger. Once you have determined to whom you are going to delegate, you will need to hone your delegating skills; there is a true art to delegation. Again, please check out the delegation chart and discussion in Chapter Four of *The Business of Design* for a description of the best approach.

The question I am asked most is: How do I go about finding someone to whom I can delegate? First, assess your current staff. If you find there are holes in their skills, you may need to either hire new people or train your current staff to perform these tasks. (It may take some effort, but training your current staff can often be far more successful than bringing in a new person who may not be the right fit for your company.) If you need to find a person because the skills do not exist in your firm, then refer to Chapter Four in this book to guide you through that process.

Here is a breakdown of the high-level responsibilities of a typical creative person and which might be delegated:

KEEP	DELEGATE	WHO MIGHT FIT THE ROLE
Firm culture	Culture buy-in	**All staff**
Project concept/vision	Project execution	**Senior designer**
Client contact	Client follow-up	**Project manager**
Financial oversight	Financial operations	**CFO/bookkeeper** *
Leadership	Management	**Senior staff**
Mentoring	Hiring/firing	**Office manager** **
Face of the firm	Marketing	**Marketing director**

* While you can hire a bookkeeper or a CFO, you still must take ultimate financial responsibility for your company.

** You must be in control of whom you hire. You do not need to find the candidates or even manage them, but you do need to know they fit into your culture. And for people who report directly to you, you cannot delegate their reviews, any disciplinary action, or dismissal.

Let's review the list on the previous page:

- **Firm culture**   The firm's environment and how it operates should be a reflection of the type of firm you want.

- **Culture buy-in**   Once you have established a culture, it is vitally important that each member of your company buy into it. For instance, if you want a culture of working hard but allowing everyone to have a balanced life, then you need to adhere to that philosophy. If you suddenly start working long hours and expect your staff to follow suit, then the culture will shift; likewise, if a senior member of your team creates a different expectation, that person's team will probably start to follow those habits and, again, the culture will shift.

- **Project concept/vision**   You want to control the overall concept and vision for each project. However, once that is articulated you can give it to your staff to carry it out. If the vision starts to shift, you may need to correct the project's course, unless you agree with that movement. This can put you more in the role of editor than executor of the design. For many principals this is their desired role, as it is efficient when faced with a large work-load. You still keep the right to veto any design or detail; options should be presented to you well in advance of any presentation to clients to allow for changes.

- **Project execution**   You can delegate a member of your team to take your design concepts and run with them. If you hand off the minutiae, you can focus on the overall design and high-level interactions with the client. A talented staff who can understand your direction and build on your ideas to create a well-thought-out design is a true gift.

- **Client contact** Most designers want to be the point of contact for their clients, but it is important to point out to clients that the project is a collaborative effort and that you are surrounded by strong people who are better suited for certain tasks.

- **Client follow-up** The more you delegate to your team, the more the client will be comfortable with the person you have put in charge of client follow-up. Remember the importance of communication; if your senior staff is communicating well with your clients, you will be dragged in less often to deal with issues that should be delegated to others.

- **Financial oversight** I can't tell you how many stories I have heard about designers who let their business be run by their CFO, business manager, or bookkeeper only to find themselves being embezzled. This was because they lost control of their financial functions—or worse, handed all control to someone else. Refer to Chapter One to fully understand which financial aspects you can delegate and which you need to stay on top of. At the end of the day you need to understand your company's finances—it is your company and this information is your power.

- **Financial operations** Again please refer to Chapter One for a detailed description of this role. But briefly, what you can delegate is the day-to-day financial management of the office. Paying the bills, sending out invoices, payroll, contracts, project management, and a whole host of other financial tasks can all be handled by your financial person. You simply need to oversee what your manager is doing and to review reports on how your company is performing on a regular basis.

- **Leadership** The leadership of your company is like the culture: you need to lead by example. The way you treat people—clients, employees, vendors—is how your staff will treat them as well. I have always said that people who are not nice to waiters are not nice people. It shows a lack of character to treat subordinates differently from peers or superiors. Some designers have a horrible reputation for the way they treat their staff; you do not want to have that reputation. Your people are your greatest asset in building and growing your firm. They will be your voice in the marketplace, and you want them to be proud of where they work.

- **Management** Leadership sets the tone and path for employees' careers and the projects they are working on, while management assembles all the right parts to move each career or project forward. Your leadership is not something you want to delegate; however, you can delegate management to the right person.

- **Mentoring** Everyone in your firm (other than the newest hire right out of school) should be mentoring someone. Your midlevel staff should mentor the junior staff; your senior staff should mentor your midlevel staff; and you should be mentoring your senior staff. We should always seek to grow and learn to keep ourselves relevant, and the art of delegating helps us to grow.

- **Hiring/firing** You can delegate the management of the staff, including hiring and firing, to your senior employees. However, if a person directly reports to you or has been in your firm for a long time, you will need to be involved in removing

"There is no fast-forward button for good service or treating your clients well. There is no technology for that, and there never will be." SUZANNE TUCKER

that person from your office. Decisions about firing are not always about poor performance; people can outgrow firms, and firms can outgrow their people. Either way, removing someone from your office should be done with dignity and understanding.

Years ago I was briefly hired by a fairly well-known designer. Only a few weeks into the engagement, I received a call insisting that I fire the firm's bookkeeper of nineteen years. Worse yet, I was asked to fire this person over the telephone. I tried to explain why this was not a good idea and that it was important for the principal of the firm to remove this person. But I was told that if I did not do this, there would be no need for us to continue working together. I replied, "If this is the way you run your business, then we are not aligned; I could not work with anyone who thinks this is acceptable." Needless to say, the engagement ended that day.

- **Face of the firm** When you are the principal of your own firm, you tend to be the one who represents the company in outside activities, promotion, and marketing. This task is rarely delegated to another person. However, if you understand that every person in your firm is an ambassador of your company, then you can mentor your staff to present your company as a great reflection of you and your values, and they, too, become the face of the firm.

- **Marketing** Marketing may require your involvement for a host of activities, such as public events or promoting a particular project, but be choosy about what activities you want to pursue. Many marketing tasks can be delegated; see Chapter Three for more insight into handling your marketing efforts.

Losing Control

Have you ever walked into your office and thought, "This is not the firm I intended to build"? I have heard people say this time and time again, usually when they first become our clients. Losing control of the firm you built is very common: one day you wake up and realize that you delegated away all the wrong parts. The culture of the firm is your responsibility—until it's not, and then the person with the strongest voice takes over. This can be a lead designer, an office manager, or even your personal assistant. You allow this person to become your gatekeeper, someone who keeps people away from you. A highly successful gatekeeper supports you and makes certain you are interacting with the people who will move your firm forward. A dysfunctional gatekeeper learns to like the power of being in control and lets his or her own vision control whom you have access to. I call this the *All About Eve* Syndrome.

We once worked with a client, an interior designer, who had let her office manager take over every aspect of running the firm. My client decided all she wanted to do was meet with clients; the rest she delegated. One day we were given the assignment of recruiting a new senior designer for her office, and we noticed that people would not return our calls once we announced the name of the designer. We began to ask why people were having such a negative reaction to this company. We learned that the firm had a reputation for doing beautiful work, but that it was a sweatshop and the office manager was impossible to work with. This was a case of a principal losing control of her company.

The culture and the vision of your firm are in your hands. Do not delegate that culture to someone else. In the end, that designer recognized she needed to take back her firm and replaced the office manager, and slowly a positive culture started to return. Now instead of dreading to come to the office, my client loves the people who work there, and they love where they work, too.

It may not always be easy to identify when you have lost control, but there are usually signs. You want to sneak in through the back door instead of announcing you have arrived; you want to work from home because you would rather be any-where else but work; or you just don't like the work that is coming out of your office anymore. All of these may seem like small issues, but they lead to a giant problem: your office is slipping out of your control. (Please remember that being in control is a good thing—the more you control, the more you can delegate and the more successful your practice will become. But being controlling is not; remember that holding anything too tightly can create failure.)

Once you identify that you have lost control and that you want to take your company back, here are a few steps toward accomplishing this task:

- First, identify why you think you have lost control. Understand the symptoms that are making you feel this way.

- Then, identify the cause: Is it a person who has taken over the control? Is it a situation that is out of hand? Are your clients or projects less inspiring than they used to be?

- Once you understand the cause, then you will need to create a solution. Let's imagine that you are not happy with a project or client and you therefore are not producing your best work. You know that if you continue to work on this project, it will not be good for the company's reputation. The solution is to remove this project from your office. How do you do this with grace and dig-nity and not create a legal issue? (My advice is always to be hon-est with clients and let them know that your vision and theirs are not philosophically aligned.)

- You will then need to think through all the consequences of your actions: Will this leave a gap in workload? Will your firm be OK financially? Will you need to lay off staff? The obstacles may seem overwhelming, so you will need to keep your eyes on the prize: regaining control of your office and regaining the joy of coming to work. If you stay focused on your goals, then you will get through the tough parts and you will be able to start enjoying your work life again.

Growth

Never grow for the sake of growing.

Many people ask me, "What is the appropriate size for my company?" The truth is that size never matters. It is all about opportunity. If projects come along that are going to move your company forward, you will probably want to take them. You ultimately want to be in a position to cherry-pick all the best projects—those that are a good fit for your firm and that you will enjoy on every level.

That said, the general rule of thumb for managing people is ten employees per leader. If you want your firm to grow, then you will need either partners or senior employees capable of managing your staff as you grow beyond those ten people. I have a client with a very large firm and only two partners, but their management team is made up of twenty-seven experienced leaders who understand the culture and leadership of the firm.

EXPANSION OF YOUR BRAND / OPENING ANOTHER OFFICE

I am often asked whether it is wise to open up an office in another city to take advantage of two different economic regions. My answer is always the same: you should never go to a new city and simply hang out your shingle. The best approach is to have a client take you to that city to see how much activity there is and whether you enjoy that marketplace. The other part of this answer is the question I always ask: Who will run that office? If you hire someone to run that office and you are not present most of the time, that office will quickly belong to that person and you run the risk that you are building a practice for this new hire. If you move a current employee to the new office, that person will bring along your culture and your methods of doing business. It is a way to elevate a key person to principal as well as helping you build a bigger firm in multiple locations. It is important to realize that you will need to be involved in growing that practice and will need to allocate time to be in that city on a regular basis.

OTHER DISCIPLINES

Many of my clients have a great interest in disciplines that are outside their education and experience. An architect may love landscape; an interior designer may love product design; or a landscape architect may love construction—any combination of interests can lead to expansion of your brand. Before you take a step like that you first need to understand its purpose. Simply to build more revenue from other services is not a good enough reason; if it is to help expand your competencies, that, too, is not a good reason. It needs to be because these additional services are aligned with your business and will expand your reach. You need to be passionate about these additional disciplines. You need to understand them, and then you need to find the best person to help you grow this business with you. Here are some tips on how to grow another discipline:

- Define the additional service you think your firm would be good at.

- Identify how that discipline will add to your practice.

- Understand the differences between your current practice and this new discipline.

- Research the marketplace and who is currently providing this service. Why will you be a better choice?

- Identify the person or people who will run this new department.

- Determine how you will market this new discipline to bring in work.

What to watch out for:

- Make certain what you are building is sustainable within your organization.

- Ensure that you are not setting someone up in business who will eventually take what you have built and start his or her own practice.

- Be careful not to alienate your peers who support your core business. For instance, if you are an architect considering building an interiors practice and a significant amount of your work comes from interior designers, then you will most likely be seen as competition and the work that is referred to you by interior designers may dry up. On the other hand, if you have clients who have no intention of hiring an interior designer but want you to do the work, then it may be wise to articulate that you only provide that service to clients who would not have hired one of your colleagues in another discipline.

- Understand thoroughly what the new discipline requires in order to perform the work on a level that is on par with your core discipline.

"The number one thing is to be passionate about what you do. You may not be passionate about how you do it, but you've got to be passionate about what you do. " **GRANT KIRKPATRICK**

Let me share a story about a firm that was not successful at adding another discipline to its practice. This took place years ago, when the economy was strong—really strong, when you could do almost anything and still bring in business. Basically, if you had a pulse, you could find work. A client told me, "I want to start a construction business along with my architectural practice." My client had a very close relationship with a general contractor who was well respected in his field but was tired of running his own practice and wanted to team up with another contractor. My client convinced this general contractor he should instead join him in his thriving architectural practice to grow both of their businesses. Because the economy was so strong, they both had enough work to keep their businesses moving through this transition. They came to terms for the acquisition and merged their practices. After almost one year to the date, the financial world collapsed and work became hard to find. Projects were being shut down, and while the architectural practice had enough work to keep going from projects that were already under construction, the construction company found itself with little or no new work. Previously, contractors had been a huge source of referrals for the architect, but now no one wanted to refer work for fear that the firm's internal contracting practice would try to take away the construction work. Meanwhile, other architects were not referring work to the general contracting division of the firm, because they were in fear of losing their work to its architectural division. Neither practice could sustain the other on the marketing efforts of the firm alone. The realization that the two firms were no longer viable was harsh.

I share this story as a cautionary tale: you must understand the path you are headed down. All that being said, there are many multidisciplinary firms that do quite well, and it is because they have established themselves well in the marketplace and they understand the pond in which they are fishing.

The Importance of Community

No one ever grew stronger living in a bubble.

Community can mean many things for each of us. Whatever your interest or your career path, it is always better to take others along for the ride. You know that saying "It's lonely at the top"? It may be a cliché, but, like many clichés, it is true. It's lonely at the top because there are many aspects of owning your own firm that are difficult to share with others. You become vulnerable if you share with your employees when they look to you for the answers; you become frustrated when you try to share your concerns with your life partner, because most of the time he or

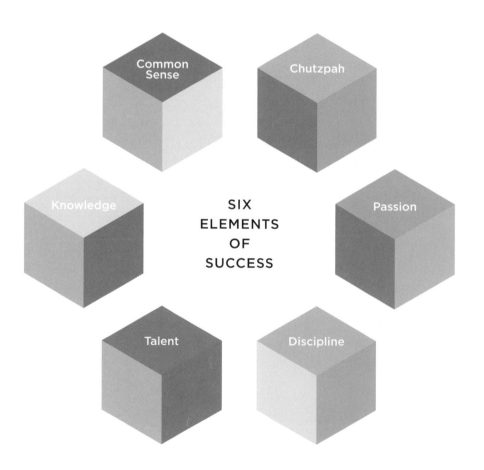

she would rather talk about anything but your business; and you really don't want to burden your friends and family with business issues that may be of no interest to them. So you need to be able to turn to a community of people who share your passion, and you can find that within your industry. Your peers are your best litmus test to help determine whether you are making the right decisions. They are your support system for future employees, future clients, and best business practices.

If you do not belong to a community, then you could start one for yourself by picking a few of your peers with whom to create regular gatherings. Years ago I cofounded the Leaders of Design Council to build community among a group of talented designers; at that time there was no place where designers could truly network with one another, sharing business concerns and resources. The mission of the group became to communicate the value of design; it has grown into a permanent organization made up of more than two hundred members. You as a leader need to find or develop your own community that brings together colleagues in your industry.

Loving Everything You Do

In closing, I would like you to think about the role that is expected of you. You are the visionary, and you need to lead your company. Your three most important responsibilities are leadership, rainmaking, and strategic thinking. All of these tasks belong to you and cannot be delegated to anyone else.

Stay clear with your vision. Always question it, and always take care of yourself both physically and mentally because without your fresh perspective your team and company will flounder. It is your job to stay relevant and to keep learning and exploring. Without that, tomorrow is not a new day—it is the same day. You deserve to wake up every day and love everything you do.

Acknowledgments

AFTER COMPLETING *The Business of Design*, I never thought there was a second book in me. But with the help of numerous people, *The Business of Creativity* came to life. I have so many individuals to thank for seeing this project come to reality.

First and foremost, I would like to thank Andrew Sessa for helping to squeeze every last word out of my brain and onto paper.

I would like to thank all the people who agreed to be interviewed for this book and shared their wisdom and experience with me. These people include Charlotte Moss, Chris Pollack, Gil Schafer, Grant Kirkpatrick, Marc Szafran, Mark Ferguson, Meg Touborg, Newell Turner, Oscar Shamamian, and Suzanne Tucker.

I would like to thank my husband, Jon, and my children, Josh and Drew, for putting up with the endless hours of isolation it took to get this project completed. My love for all three of you is boundless. Thanks as well to all my family and friends who have supported me not only during the writing of this book but with every crazy idea I come up with on a daily basis.

By my side for so many years is the incomparable Christine Tope. You are my air traffic controller and my career rock, and for your loyalty and commitment I am forever grateful.

At Princeton Architectural Press, thanks to Kevin Lippert, Jennifer Lippert, Sara Stemen, Paul Wagner, Benjamin English, Janet Behning, Lia Hunt, and Jaime Nelson Noven for your support and guidance, which have allowed us to create this beautiful book.

Like my first book, *The Business of Creativity* is only seeing the light of day because of the skills and guidance of Jill Cohen. You are my friend and my colleague, and I adore you.

Every year I feed my soul through my work at the Leaders of Design Council. I am as proud of this work as I am honored to share the leadership with my partner, Meg Touborg. Meg and I would be worthless without the support and guidance of Dana Colla, who makes magic appear every day in her dedication to the organization.

My career has taken many paths but always has been pointed toward helping the design profession become stronger. With that in mind, I want to acknowledge all the people behind DesignersAxis; together we will revolutionize the interior design industry. Many thanks to my partner, Lance Haeberle, for your absolute genius and insight, and our team: Wallene Reimer, Chris Wilson, Sarah Walsh, and Robert Stone. I would like to also thank our board, Tom Stringer, Lisa and Cary Kravet, and Shana Fisher, for your guidance and sage advice. And to all the investors who believed in us to make this dream a reality.

I am a blessed man to live a life I treasure on a daily basis, and I was given that life and the drive to succeed by my mother, Dorothy Granet. I love you with all my heart and thank you every day for your unconditional love and support. Lastly, Marianne Nelson, you make my life brighter by your support and love.